A Companion to *The Crying of Lot 49*

A COMPANION TO

The Crying of Lot 49

J. KERRY GRANT

The University of Georgia Press

Athens and London

© 1994 by the University of Georgia Press
Athens, Georgia 30602
All rights reserved

Set in Trump Mediaeval by Tseng Information Systems, Inc.
Printed and bound by Thomson-Shore, Inc.
The paper in this book meets the guidelines for
permanence and durability of the Committee on
Production Guidelines for Book Longevity of the
Council on Library Resources.

Printed in the United States of America

04 03 02 01   P   8   7   6   5

Library of Congress Cataloging in Publication Data

Grant, J. Kerry.
A companion to The crying of lot 49 / J. Kerry Grant.
p.   cm.
Includes bibliographical references and index.
ISBN 0-8203-1635-0 (alk. paper). — ISBN 0-8203-1636-9
(pbk. : alk. paper)
1. Pynchon, Thomas. Crying of lot 49.   I. Title.
PS3566.Y55C792   1994
813'.54—dc20   93–38157

British Library Cataloging in Publication Data available

For Jean and Ian Grant

Contents

⚊◁◫ Acknowledgments

Thanks are due to St. Lawrence University for the opportunity to devote a year to this project. Portions of the commentary on Pynchon's use of entropy and Maxwell's Demon have appeared in *Pynchon Notes* 28–29 (Spring-Fall 1991): 43–53. I thank the editors of that journal for their support.

Thank you, too, to colleagues who answered some odd questions and offered good advice. Particular thanks to Steven White, whose subtle translations shed a great deal of light, and to Sandy Hinchman, who read some early pages with much care.

Any errors and omissions are my own. My thanks to Steven Weisenburger, whose detailed comments helped me avoid some fairly egregious ones.

⌐◁] Introduction

Ask most people who Thomas Pynchon is and chances are they will either have no idea or they will identify him as the author of *The Crying of Lot 49*. They may be able to name some or all of his other works, but most are unlikely to have read them, even in college literature courses.

For those readers who were exposed to Pynchon in college, the reasoning behind this state of affairs is not hard to deduce. Pynchon, so goes the thinking, is a hugely talented and innovative writer who has made such a name for himself that ignoring his work would be inappropriate; however, the stories in *Slow Learner* have been dismissed as apprentice work, both *V.* and *Gravity's Rainbow* are much too long and complex for the average reader, and *Vineland* is too recent to have attracted a reliable safety net of critical commentary for the nervous instructor to fall back on. *Lot 49*, on the other hand, has been taken very seriously by critics, it is appealingly brief, with something resembling a linear plot and a stable point of view, and there is a plethora of secondary material. At the same time, the novel offers a relatively painless introduction to some of the characteristics of literary postmodernism and affords a glimpse of Pynchon's unique imagination, his enthusiasm for scientific metaphors, his concern for the fate of losers and schlemiels, his satirical vision of contemporary America, etc., etc.

And so, each year, thousands of students are introduced to the novel and, I'm willing to bet, each year a substantial number of them come away from the experience, despite the best efforts of their instructors, convinced that Pynchon is too difficult—too weird, too clever, too something—for them. This is certainly my experience of teaching *Lot 49*, and my colleagues assure me it is theirs also.

The fact is, of course, that there is much to be baffled by in *The Crying of Lot 49*. Imagine, for example, attempting to compose brief responses to the following questions or directives:

1. Distinguish between thermodynamic and informational entropy and explain their roles in the novel.
2. Distinguish clearly between "inside" and "outside," between "safe" and "lost," as you try to explain Oedipa's meditation on metaphor.
3. Just what is the "high magic to low puns" that makes significant the congruence between delirium tremens and delta-t?
4. Is paranoia healthy or destructive?
5. Is the novel finally sacred or profane?
6. Do the previous two questions represent a dubious commitment to binary thinking? Explain why or why not.
7. Are excluded middles always "bad shit"?

I am confident that many readers of *Lot 49* would experience at least some difficulty with this assignment, which, in my opinion, directs attention to some of the novel's central concerns. Even after a number of readings, the novel resists interpretation to an extraordinary degree, especially if "interpretation" is taken to mean the effort to tease out a unitary and more or less comprehensive account of the novel's message from the tangled network of metaphor and allusion that is Pynchon's trademark. Notwithstanding the strictures of poststructuralist theory (see, in particular, McHoul and Wills), such an effort remains the first inclination of most readers, and it is often only after repeated failures that the novel's tendency to frustrate and redirect the impulse begins to seem innate, rather than simply the result of incomplete or defective reading strategies.

Critical commentary, then, can be categorized according to its willingness to accept this aspect of the novel. At one end of the spectrum we find those who, like Debra Castillo, seem willing to contemplate total openness: "What happens," she asks, "if we as readers

conceive of the narrative as a progressive and strictly uninterpret-
able distortion rather than as a jumble of zeros and ones from which
the critic, like Maxwell's Demon, sorts true from false, inside from
outside, hot from cold, relevant from nonsensical? What if we were
to make no claim to understand the linguistic forces and movements
of *The Crying of Lot 49*, but merely to read the ion trails of their
passage?" (39). The opposite extreme is characterized by claims such
as Robert N. Watson's, that the novel "is a coherent book, with an
ethical message underlying its narrative shape and its theological
analogies, rather than merely a cluster of amusing games, patterns,
and allusions" (59). One critic confidently asserts that "language as
a mirror of reality or as a medium capable of establishing significant
contacts beyond its own closed system is profoundly denied in Pynchon's fiction" (Leland 49), while another notes the "sheer density"
of the novel's references to "the world as we know it" (Nicholson
and Stevenson 95). Where Thomas Hill Schaub sees an uncertainty
that is introduced "into every perception allowed to Oedipa and the
reader" (21), claiming that "the text itself oscillates like a standing
wave between nodes of meaning" (24), Edward Mendelson, before
Schaub was able to persuade him otherwise, was able to see in the
novel's religious imagery a set of "processes" that point toward coherence and "community" (114). The novel has been read both as an
"exemplary postmodern text" (Castillo 39) and as a parody of postmodernist interpretive strategies (David Bennett 38).

Such oppositions are scarcely surprising, given the novel's own
preoccupation, in its closing stages, with binary choices. As might
be supposed, also, efforts to accommodate the many polarities that
the novel introduces abound. Like Oedipa herself, critics have apparently heard that "excluded middles" are not such a good thing, and
so their concern is to identify some form of middle ground for the
reader to occupy. Frank Palmeri, for example, asserts that Pynchon
has produced "a text that signifies neither literally nor metaphorically" (980), and that he "uses puns, as he uses entropy, to think about
the paradigms [entropy, the Tristero, the myth of Narcissus] rather
than within them, and to signal our position between inaccessible
fullness and profane emptiness of meaning" (985). Pynchon "situ-

ates his novel between tragedy and satire, parody and allegory" (995). This view is similar to Tony Tanner's, which is rooted in that moment in *The Courier's Tragedy* when "a gentle chill, an ambiguity, begins to creep in among the words" and "a new mode of expression takes over" (*Thomas Pynchon* 71). Tanner, like Palmeri, sees this "new mode" as existing "between the literal and the metaphorical" (*Thomas Pynchon* 59). Finally, for Dwight Eddins, the novel's "problematic" is constituted by its "religio-secular binaries," and he argues that "if there is a way out . . . it would seem to involve the retention, somehow, of both 'transcendent meaning' *and* a recalcitrant earth, a ground of apeirontic chaos; and with that duality we are returned to the concept of the *metaxy* . . . an in-between in which humanity is to some degree illuminated by spiritual possibility without losing its base in the opaque materiality of natural process" (91).

Even as brief a survey as this may serve to reinforce what readers already know, namely that *Lot 49* elicits complex and contradictory responses which can scarcely be satisfactorily accommodated by a single essay or a chapter in a book. The texture of the novel is so dense, its allusiveness so pronounced, its tone so varied, that only the perspective afforded by multiple readings can begin to serve the needs of the conscientious reader. The annotations and observations that follow, therefore, are offered in a pragmatic spirit as a guide for those who wish to elaborate on their own readings of the novel, and they are organized in such a way as to resist the imposition of any single interpretive strategy.

At the same time, however, it would be foolish to pretend that I myself have no particular "take" on the novel, and that the choices informing each note or comment are unconnected to such a general interpretation. I have been reading and teaching *The Crying of Lot 49* for almost twenty years and can scarcely have avoided developing a way of understanding the book itself as well as the commentary that has grown up around it. While I have not consciously excluded readings that I may not personally endorse, I have no doubt that certain biases in favor of my own range of assumptions will be detectable by the discerning reader.

With this in mind, I offer by way of preface to the main body of this work a brief account of what I have come to regard as the novel's major preoccupations.

At the heart of the novel lies Pynchon's concern with our culture's movement toward intellectual inertia. Oedipa's quest is essentially a search for a source of energy that will revitalize her life and the lives of those who live in mainstream America. Because the culture of which she is a representative is envisaged as a closed system in which the available resources are gradually being used up, she must look beyond the established boundaries of her world if she is to discover a genuinely new energy source. The Mexican anarchist, Jesús Arrabal (see H119.10n), provides a key phrase when he describes a miracle as "another world's intrusion into this one" (H120.7), adding another link to a chain of associations with the concept of revelation that the novel forges. Oedipa's liberation from her Rapunzel-like life in Kinneret exposes her to the possibility of revelation, sensitizing her to the potential existence of "the direct, epileptic Word, the cry that might abolish the night" (H118.16n). The novel's use of the language of religious belief serves to reinforce our sense that Oedipa may be receiving input from outside the confines of the day-to-day, input that could provide the cure for the "unvarying gray sickness" (H14.24) that infects the whole culture and not just the part of it that Mucho is exposed to in his car lot.

Oedipa, however, finds herself unable to determine whether the revelations that come crowding in on her are genuinely intrusions from some other realm of meaning and possibility, or whether they are simply the manifestations of Pierce's own desire to avoid the inertia of death. By the end of the novel, Oedipa is almost paralyzed by her dilemma, apparently trapped in a world that has resolved itself into a set of binary opposites, an either/or equilibrium that is the antithesis of the advice that Pierce had once given her: "Keep it bouncing" (H178.30). Nevertheless, her willingness to attend the auction attests to the fact that she has not entirely given up her quest, and the fact that the novel closes before any definitive answer is given to the question of the Tristero's existence allows us to understand that she remains open, despite her exhaustion, to the further enlargement of her world.

In *Lot 49*, Pynchon exposes the radical uncertainties that underlie our attempts to discern meaning in the signs that come crowding in on us every minute of our lives. As Oedipa discovers, too much information can leave the individual just as powerless as too little. The novel charts a wavering course between the nihilism of Mucho's "N.A.D.A." dream (H144.22n) and the total determinism of the possibility that Pierce has created the whole Tristero network. Where we might have expected to find stable symbolic structures, therefore, we find shifting patterns of association and significance. Thus, the Tristero is sometimes seen as the champion of the world's disinherited, a "real alternative to . . . exitlessness" (H170.25), and sometimes it is envisaged as a dark, sinister force, motivated by its own desire for control and imperialistic dominion. Similarly, as Schaub points out, the novel's main figurative device, the concept of entropy, is inherently ambivalent, pointing in one direction to stagnation and inertia, via thermodynamics, and in the other to potential richness of communication, via information theory (21). The reader is inexorably caught up in Oedipa's predicament precisely because the experience of reading the novel so closely resembles her efforts to disentangle Pierce's legacy.

Like Oedipa, then, the reader may want to project a world—a world in which the novel's inherent ambiguity is somehow not destructive of enjoyment, not merely frustrating, but part of the very "secret richness and concealed density of dream" that it seeks to rediscover for us. I hope that the notes that follow can be used as a means to that end.

My primary purpose has been to loosen some of the novel's interpretive tangles by reproducing critical commentary on specific details and by offering commentary of my own. Rather than simply refer the reader to a particular essay or critic, I have quoted or paraphrased key passages from the secondary literature with the deliberate aim in mind of saving the busy (and perhaps not altogether obsessed) reader time in her/his pursuit of some understanding of this complex work.

While the majority of the notes are interpretive in nature, some are designed simply to recover for today's reader what may have proved ephemeral in the way of references to popular culture, or to fill in historical background that may be helpful.

References are keyed to the Perennial Library Edition of the novel, published in 1986 by Harper and Row, and to the Bantam edition, published in 1967. I have followed the format adopted by Steven Weisenburger in his *Gravity's Rainbow Companion* (1988). Thus page and line numbers for the two editions are given in boldface along with the item that is the subject of the note. Cross references are provided in parentheses and direct the reader either to other pages in the novel or, when the citation is accompanied by an "n," to other annotations.

A Companion to *The Crying of Lot 49*

Chapter 1

H9.1, B1.1 Mrs Oedipa Maas Few commentaries on the novel are silent on the subject of Oedipa's name. Most take for granted that it is significant in a straightforward way: by referring the reader to some extratextual network of meanings the name appropriates some or all of those meanings for the novel, which thus draws part of its own significance from the resonances they generate. This is the "conventional" response that at least one critic claims is unavoidable. Moddelmog maintains that even if the name is a joke, the only way to determine that fact is by "answering the question 'Is Oedipa Oedipal?' "(240). Moddelmog calls into question the claim that Pynchon's names are meaningful only in the sense that they expose the dangers of our willingness to read meaning into them. This view is forcefully expressed by Tanner: "In Pynchon's texts names do not operate as they do in, for example, Fielding in which Thwackum or Allworthy are—or do—exactly what their names indicate. . . . 'Character' and identity are not stable in his fiction, and the wild names he gives his 'characters,' which seem either to signify too much (Oedipus and Newton indeed!) or too little (like comic-strip figures), are a gesture against the tyranny of naming itself. Lacan sees the fact that we are *named* before we can speak as a symptom of the degree to which we are at the mercy of language itself. Pynchon indicates that he can see how, in various ways, people are subject to the authority of naming" ("Crying" 178). Mac Adam makes a little less of the same point: "Pynchon's onomastic punning produces a kind of Brechtian 'alienation effect,' reminding the reader that what he is reading is a fiction, that the words here are only words" (560). Caesar, whom Tanner cites approvingly, also occupies the minority camp, arguing for the "frivolousness" of Pynchon's naming practices. " 'Maas,' " Caesar claims, "can be voiced to sound like 'my ass'; this Oedipa is no Oedipus, or only one at the earnest reader's peril" (5).

There are, it would seem, a lot of earnest readers out there. The association of Oedipa with the Sophoclean Oedipus is almost a leitmotif of critical writing on the novel, with Freud coming in a close second. Moddelmog is unequivocal in her conclusion: "Despite cosmological variances between their worlds, the general pattern of Oedipus's and Oedipa's lives is identical: during their investigations, both characters move away from absolute positivism to relative indeterminacy; the 'crime' that both find so appalling is that they were so self-absorbed that they never saw the danger of the former position" (248). This view is echoed in Nicholson: "Like her namesake in Thebes, Oedipa discovers that a determination to reduce the riddling complexity of her experience to satisfyingly rational and unitary conclusions is one that only brings trouble on herself" (107). And by Mendelson: "The name . . . refers back to the Sophoclean Oedipus who begins his search for the solution of a problem (a problem, like Oedipa's, involving a dead man) as an almost detached observer, only to discover how deeply implicated he is in what he finds" (118). The idea of Oedipus as detective fuels further associations with Oedipa's quest, some of them suggesting a congruence between "Sophocles' solver of riddles" (Nicholson 93) and Pynchon's California housewife, while others note discrepancies that either negate the association or complicate it in the direction of irony or parody. Tanner points out that Oedipus's riddle has to do with "parents, parricide and incest" and that this "in no way applies to Oedipa" ("Crying" 178). Palmeri acknowledges that the name "echoes Freud and Sophocles," but dismisses Freud on Oedipus as a "red herring" (994), and notes that "Oedipa withdraws from the role of detective who uncovers what has been hidden. Unlike Oedipus, who sees the riddle of his own identity hidden under his answer to the Sphinx's riddle, Oedipa remains unenlightened"

(995). Newman claims that the "generally symbolic associations" that accumulate around Oedipa's name are "simultaneously deflated by the ordinariness of her suburban existence" (69), and of course we have already noted Caesar's reading of the name.

Freudian associations run the gamut from the relatively complex to the more or less straightforward. Couturier, citing Christopher Lasch's description of "the devouring mother of pre-Oedipal fantasy," sees Oedipa's conception of herself as the female in the tower as an image of "this castrating mother," who, "by a strange process of poetic reversal (which Freud tells us is frequently present in dreams) . . . has been given the feminized name of her docile son, Oedipus." Couturier supposes that Pierce, feeling himself diminished by Oedipa's inaccessibility, may have sought revenge "by burdening her with an ego-destructive task" (22). Plater wonders if the feminization of Oedipus is intended to "suggest the hermaphroditic unity of opposites, which Freud saw as the goal of the human body, as it struggles to overcome the dualities of life and death" (150–51). Coates claims that "*The Crying of Lot 49* is an attempt to bring the American consciousness, personified in Oedipa Maas (nothing is more American than Freudianism), to an awareness of all it has repressed" (125). Hite remarks that Oedipa's name is "initially merely ludicrous," but that it "loses its associations with Freudian trendiness as the quest proceeds, and begins to recall her truth-seeking Sophoclean predecessor" (74). Finally, Cowart notes in passing that "Oedipa" is "a suitably neurotic name" ("Varo" 20).

A few other readings of the name seem worth noting. Tanner refers to "Maas" as having been associated with Newton's second law of motion "in which 'mass' is the term denoting a quantity of inertia" ("Crying" 178). Davidson goes further afield: "Significantly, her married name, 'Maas,' is the Afrikaans word for 'web' or 'net' and, as such, perfectly describes her situation—someone trapped in various intermingling mazes and meshes" (43). Chambers takes us in the other direction when she points out that "in Dutch 'Maas' means 'mesh' or 'stitch' and is an idiom for 'to slip through the meshes and find an avenue of escape' " (101).

In this connection it is worth noting that the third panel of the Varo triptych that Oedipa recalls seeing in Mexico City denotes the maiden's escape from the tower where her companions are embroidering their tapestry of the world (H21.1n). Colville cites P.-Y. Petillon's association of the name with the Dutch *Maaswerk*, "which means the woof or background threads through which the warp is woven and which forms the hidden part of the tapestry" (12).

H9.2, B1.2 Tupperware party Part of what Hite refers to as the "hyperbolically banalized world" (73) of the novel's opening. While Kermode is not exactly expansive on the significance of the apparently surprising fact that "on these occasions goods are sold outside the normal commercial system" (11), the context suggests that he sees the Tupperware party as evidence of a world in which "everybody is tending toward his own dissident universe of meaning" (12). Given Tupperware's association with middle-class suburban life, this seems a touch farfetched. Couturier has more to say on the subject: "It is not the airtight containers which are really for sale but a little share of conviviality. No medium is being used, except money, the medium par excellence. Money is what prevents genuine exchange between the guests at such parties; it pollutes everybody's speech. The hostess must resort to an extreme solution to make her guests relax and buy goods: she gets them drunk on Kirsch. This is not a real party, therefore, but a simulacrum of a party" (13).

H9.4, B1.4 executor . . . executrix Evidence, for Couturier, of "the freakish manipulation of the characters' sexual identities" (24). He supposes that the letter has used the masculine form and that she supplies the feminine as an indication of her resentment at the inaccuracy. I think, however, it is more logical to assume that the letter uses neither word, since there would be no reason for her to "suppose" that it had named her executrix if in fact it had used the word "executor." Oedipa surely supplies both forms, correcting her own instinctive first use of the masculine form in favor of what she takes to be the more appropriate or perhaps simply the conventionally "correct" feminine. One might note in passing that the suggestion of feminist irritation here is at odds with our early image of Oedipa as self-professed Young Republican, the "slight . . . little housewife" (Henkle 106) who only gradually "leaves the limits of her socialization" to experience "a change of consciousness" (Kolodny and Peters 82).

H9.5, B1.5 Pierce Inverarity Again, one of Pynchon's tantalizingly suggestive names. The critics have had a field day with this one. Kermode and Tanner are in agreement about the name's equivocal significance, suggesting that it (or its owner) "may be either un-truth or *dans le vrai*" (Kermode 11), or, to put it the same way, that it "can suggest either un-truth or in-the-truth" (Tanner, "Crying" 176). Tanner also notes that he has seen the name glossed as "pierces or peers into variety" ("Crying" 176). Poirier appears to earn the credit for turning up a "real-life stamp collector named Pierce," and for noting that the kind of stamps that make up Lot 49 would be known in the business as "inverse rarities" (22). This last observation might be wishful thinking, however, since no mention of the expression appears in the American Philatelic Society's *Fundamentals of Philately*, whose glossary includes only "inversions" and "inverted center/frame" as types of oddity. David Bennett suggests that, because Pierce is "omnipresent and invisible," he is "the inverse of rarity" (37). Schaub's assertion that Inverarity is the birthplace of James Clerk Maxwell, whose demon looms large in the novel (H86.3n), would be at least intriguing, if it were true. In fact, Inverarity is at least forty miles from the street in Edinburgh where Maxwell was born, so we might want to find another reason for thinking of Pierce as "the demon of his own system" (Schaub 29).

Perhaps because of that "high magic to low puns" that the novel asserts, Schaub's interpretive footing seems surer when he associates Pierce, via Peter, with "petrus" or rock (33). He is joined by Newman, who describes Pierce as "a type of profane Peter" whose "perverse church is a secular conglomerate" (75). For Schaub, Pierce is "an inverse Peter, on whom is built the profane church of America" (33).

Mac Adam claims that Inverarity represents the artist. "His

given name, Pierce . . . evok[es] the phallic stylus violating the white purity of the page, while his last name, Inverarity, hints at such concepts as inveracity and inversion, the illusory or lying aspects of writing" (563).

H9.9, B1.8   sorting it all out   The question of what "sorting" actually entails is brought up later in the novel on a couple of occasions and extended commentary on it is thus deferred until the appropriate moment. It is worth noting, however, that Oedipa's engagement with the "tangled" assets of Pierce's estate is frequently said to be equivalent to the reader's engagement with the novel. We, like Oedipa, embark on a quest for clarity and discover a world that both appeals to and resists our instinctive tendency to seek order. Of course, we have been well prepared for this analogy. The peculiar mixture of pleasure and frustration that readers of *V.* experience owes much to the fact that it constantly reminds us how eager we are to make connections, to pin the novel down to a final, unifying explanation, while at the same time making fun of that impulse. As Stencil capers along after V., we follow along as best we can, wondering all the while whether, in the eyes of some cosmic onlooker, we are not as clownish as he. In *Lot 49*, Pynchon continues to tantalize and frustrate us as we follow Oedipa through the labyrinth of Pierce's legacy, trying, like her, to distinguish signal from noise and no doubt in the process getting the two hopelessly mixed up.

While Oedipa sorts through the myriad clues afforded by the will and its secondary effects, we observe over her shoulder and do our best to make connections. Baxter identifies Oedipa's difficulty in terms that seem relevant to our predicament as readers: "In *The Crying of Lot 49*, the legacy has been so hopelessly tangled that to sort it out . . . seems a virtually obsolescent activity. 'Sorting' implies clear categories, and categories suggest some kind of sure epistemological methodology; but there is no such certainty here, not even the suggestion of one" (28). This view is echoed by Seed, who ascribes to Oedipa a kind of "epistemic bewilderment caused by the deluge of information to which she is subjected" (134). Pynchon, we are reminded again and again, is acutely conscious of the fact that we live in an age of uncertainty, an age in which in-determinacy is a fundamental component of our understanding of matter. Sorting, therefore, is inevitably a problematic activity.

H9.10, B1.9 the greenish dead eye of the TV tube A "communica-tion system with no message" (Kermode 11), the blank television is glossed by Tanner as a substitute for true religion ("Crying" 179). Couturier sees the juxtaposition of "God" and the TV as an appeal for help to the media (6). Schaub is more ambitious, claim-ing that "the TV's 'greenish eye' [sic] becomes the green bubble shades nearly everyone wears, and which, like the TV, permit the wearer to be in someone else's living space without making con-tact" (33). As far as I can determine, Oedipa is the only character ever described as wearing "green bubble shades," although sev-eral other characters—Metzger, Manny Di Presso, the associates of Tony Jaguar who are chasing him—are seen wearing "shades" at various times.

H9.11, B1.10 spoke the name of God This is the starting point for a significant debate about the novel's religious attributes. Mendel-son, whose essay is almost certainly the best-known exposition of religious themes in *Lot 49*, counts this as the first of "per-haps twenty"—actually, there are thirty-three—uses of the word "God" in the book. This "quiet but insistent echo," this "muted but audible signal" (126–27), is a component of the novel's overall preoccupation with the sacred, according to Mendelson, who in-sists that "religious meaning is itself the central issue of the plot" (120). Others either explicitly or implicitly endorse this view, vari-ously describing Oedipa's use of the name of God as "religious imagery" (Newman 74), "thoughts about God" (Kermode 11), and a "significant response [that] is repeated twice in contexts of reve-lation" (Nohrnberg 149). Tanner, on the other hand, finds little promise of the sacred in Oedipa's appeal to what has become "an empty word" ("Crying" 179). This is the closest thing I have seen to a recognition of the possibility that "spoke the name of God" may be mock portentous. After all, we can very easily visualize the scene, in which a slightly drunken Oedipa is faced with a reminder not only of her relationship with Pierce but also of his death, a reminder that brings with it the promise of complications, perturbations in the even flow of her suburban existence. "Oh, God," or something like it, scarcely seems like an excessive expletive under the circumstances, nor does it seem endowed with anything but commonplace secular resonances.

H10.1, B1.11 this did not work One of Tanner's "three substitutes for true religion in the contemporary world" ("Crying" 179), the others being the TV and the name of God, Oedipa's attempt to feel drunk is indicative of her desire to insulate herself against the implications of the task that now faces her. That it does not work is perhaps an indication of the fact that she is beginning, in Hite's fanciful image, to rise "like Venus emerging from the sea . . . from a 'Californicated' level of existence into a new life" (73).

H10.2, B1.12 a hotel room in Mazatlán Presumably a memory from her time in Mexico with Pierce. Mazatlán is situated on the western coast of Mexico, some six hundred miles northwest of Mexico City. The slamming of the door suggests that Oedipa's relationship with Pierce ended on a sour note, and now Metzger's letter has come to reopen that chapter in her life.

H10.4, B1.14 sunrise over the library slope As an undergraduate at Cornell, Pynchon would have had many an opportunity not to see the sunrise on the library slope. The echo here of the old conundrum concerning the tree in the forest is given a typically wry Pynchonian twist when one considers that sunrise is not the busiest time on any college campus and that library slopes, westward facing or otherwise, are not likely to be heavily populated at such a time. A number of readers assume that this memory makes Oedipa a Cornell graduate, but the novel's only other reference to Oedipa's education would seem to suggest otherwise (H103.32n).

H10.6, B1.16 a dry, disconsolate tune Cowart suggests that the tune "may be an intimation of impending disorder," citing Pynchon's use of Bartók in "Mortality and Mercy in Vienna" as a possible catalyst for a character's running amok (*Art of Allusion* 78).

H10.8, B1.18 bust of Jay Gould The bust, according to Fowler, "[symbolizes] the purity of [Pierce's] lineage back to the great 19th Century robber barons" (10). Jay Gould (1836–92) was an unscrupulous railroad entrepreneur, noted for the shadiness of his business transactions. The implied comparison never receives explicit endorsement in the novel, which offers no evidence that Pierce was actually dishonest in his dealings.

H10.15, B2.7 Warpe, Wistfull, Kubitschek and McMingus Certainly not Pynchon's most extravagantly named law firm, but a good warm-up for the Hobbesian "Salitieri, Poore, Nash, De Brutus, and Short" of *Gravity's Rainbow* fame.

H10.17, B2.9 Metzger Nicholson cites Mendelson's note that the name is German for butcher and then adds his own observation: "Because of the peripatetic nature of their trade, German butchers in the Middle Ages were given letters to carry from village to village: Metzger hence came to signify 'temporary postman' "(94). The "butcher post" was by no means an exclusively medieval phenomenon, however: "In the course of time the Butchers' Guild formed a regular postal organization. A patent of the Emperor Rudolf II in 1597 mentions the butcher post as an established institution to promote communication. Even in 1622, after the beginning of the Thirty Years' War, a special Post and Butcher Regulation issued by Duke Johann Friedrich of Wurttemburg shows that in remote localities where there was no regular mail service the butchers were still in the habit of carrying letter bags. . . . For a long time these German butchers had been in the habit of carrying a bugle with which to announce their arrival to buy cattle, and this now became in some sense a post horn. Even in the nineteenth century the butchers' guilds often had a bugle in their coats of arms. In Wurttemburg they continued to use the bugle until the end of the seventeenth century, and the Thurn and Taxis officials frequently complained bitterly of the butchers using what they called the 'post horn' " (Harlow 67).

The chain of associations forged by these connected observations makes for an interesting ambiguity in our attitude toward Metzger. His name links him by analogy to competitors of the Thurn and Taxis organization, and hence to the Tristero, a fact that accords well with Watson's thesis, which maintains that through the Tristero Oedipa comes to the brink of self-discovery, after being rescued by Metzger from her "comfortable and complacent" suburban life (61). Metzger, however, is Pierce Inverarity's legal representative and thus is closely associated with the main current of American capitalism—the equivalent of the monopolistic Thurn and Taxis dynasty. This latter suggestion has ties to the speculations raised by the discovery that W.A.S.T.E. stands for "We Await Silent Tristero's Empire," an anticipation of the time when the Tristero itself will take over the monopolistic functions of the state system (169).

H10.18, B2.10   just now found the will   "One satiric convention . . . is the lost and recovered manuscript, which provides a formal explanation for satire's lacunae, problematic authority or authorship, unverifiability, and incompleteness. This convention of the satiric *apocryphon* appears in *Lot 49* as the last will and testament of Inverarity" (Nohrnberg 157).

H10.23, B2.15   Through the rest of the afternoon   This whole passage is oddly misrepresented by Tanner: "We first encounter Oedipa Maas among the eclectic bric-a-brac of contemporary Californian culture, buying lasagne and *Scientific American* in shops that indifferently play Muzak or Vivaldi" ("Crying" 177).

   Tanner has the general tone right, of course, having clearly inferred, like almost everyone else who takes note of the passage, that Oedipa's life is banal and predictable, a not-quite parody of a middle-class suburban routine that we know is going to be destroyed by the quest that has just been inaugurated.

H10.25, B2.16   Kinneret-Among-The-Pines   Watson notes that "Lake Kinneret was an alternative name for the Sea of Galilee" (67).

H10.25, B2.17   to buy ricotta and listen to the Muzak   Tyson suggests that this moment typifies Oedipa's immersion in a world marked by "a profusion of empty commodity-signs, signs that mark an absence rather than a presence—an absence of art, of history, of myth—and therefore require no existential engagement" (8–9).

H10.29, B2.20   Vivaldi Kazoo Concerto   Cowart reminds us that the concerto surfaces in *V.*, where Profane meets a "musicologist who had devoted his life to finding the lost Vivaldi Kazoo Concerto" (*Art of Allusion* 79), evidently with some success.

H11.3, B2.27   Wendell ("Mucho") Maas   Davidson is not alone in pointing out that Mucho's extramarital flings with his pubescent listeners indicate the name's association with "macho" (43). This weakness of Mucho's anticipates Nefastis's enthusiasm for "young stuff" (H105.3), and Metzger's "Humbert Humbert" disappearing act (H147.6n). The whole complex of associations reminds us of Pynchon's frequent depiction of the "nymphet" figure: Nerissa in "Low-lands," Fina in *V.*, Bianca in *Gravity's Rainbow*. Mucho will put in another appearance as a reformed coke addict in *Vineland*.

H11.6, B2.30   more or less identical   The first inkling of one of the novel's major themes. Oedipa's life in Kinneret has been without variety; it resembles the cultural heat-death predicted by Callisto in Pynchon's story "Entropy," in which a "tendency from . . . differentiation to sameness" would result in the cessation of "intellectual motion" (283). Note, by the way, that a strict adherence to such a reading depends on our making invidious distinctions between the book reviews and the other articles in the *Scientific American* she obviously subscribes to. Clearly, some kind of intellectual exchange is occurring; it is up to the reader how condescending she wants to be at this early stage about Oedipa's willingness to absorb new and significant information.

H11.9, B2.32   Huntley and Brinkley   Chet Huntley (1911–74) and David Brinkley (b. 1920) were co-anchors of NBC's nightly news report from 1956 to 1970.

H11.12, B2.36   a voice beginning   Green associates Pierce with Conrad's Kurtz (see H11.18n). He might also have noted a further connection in the fact that our only link with the living Pierce is through this voice. Marlow's knowledge of Kurtz is from the beginning associated with a sense of the man's voice.

"This call already defines Pierce, the originator of Oedipa's quest, as a mere compound and reflection of various cultural icons and a switchboard of various discursive frameworks. . . . Pierce is not an original person but a cultural simulacrum" (Berressem 89).

H11.15, B2.38   hostile Pachuco dialect   "Pachuco" was the name given to a certain subgroup of Hispanic Americans in the thirties and forties. The forerunners of today's urban gang members, they wore zoot suits and spoke a mixed English/Spanish slang, here characterized by the obscenities "fuck" and "faggot" ("chinga," "maricones").

HII.18, B3.1 Lamont Cranston The best-known alter ego of radio's Shadow, though not the only one, apparently. Each week the show's announcer reminded listeners that "the Shadow, mysterious character who aids the forces of law and order, is in reality Lamont Cranston, wealthy young man-about-town. Several years ago in the Orient, Cranston learned a strange and mysterious secret . . . the hypnotic power to cloud men's minds so they cannot see him" (Buxton and Owen 313).

Guzlowski lists a number of the character's other putative "real" selves, implying that, by association, Pierce's own identity becomes less defined, more shadowy (61). "The Shadow" had a twenty-year run on radio, starting in the early thirties, and the mysterious eponymous hero was played by a number of actors, among them Orson Welles. By way of trivial coincidence, note the following: "The invisible effect was created aurally and psychologically by putting Cranston's voice through a filter that made it sound like a telephone conversation" (Sterling and Kittross 121).

A number of critics have commented on Pierce's choice of the Lamont Cranston voice, linking the mysteriousness of the Shadow to the ambiguities that Oedipa confronts in the course of her quest. Pearce, for example, notes that "Pierce Inverarity is introduced as a shadow undergoing continual transformation" (222), while Abernethy asserts that the "ambiguous nature" of Pierce's will "is indicated by [his] last disguise, that of Lamont Cranston, the 'Shadow' " (19). Nohrnberg derives a religious connotation that finds an echo in Watson's reading of the novel's ending as a version of the Annunciation (see H183.14n). "Although she is not in the least virginal, Oedipa's story receives a Marian configuration from the moment that Pierce Inverarity . . . telephones his promise to the heroine that 'the Shadow' will be paying her a visit (cf. Luke 1:35: 'The Holy Spirit will overshadow thee')" (11). The stickler for detail will note, however, that Pierce threatens Mucho, not Oedipa, with a visit from the Shadow.

Green's association of Pierce with Conrad's Kurtz permits a more psychoanalytic reading: "Pierce is indeed a shadow cast over much of Oedipa's life and over all the clues to Tristero; but he is also, as Kurtz is to Marlow, an alter ego to her, a shadow in a Jungian sense" (35).

H11.22, B3.5 Margo Pynchon appears to have misspelled the name. According to Buxton and Owen's version of the script: "Cranston's friend and companion, the lovely Margot Lane, is the only person who knows to whom the voice of the invisible Shadow belongs" (313).

H11.23, B3.5 Commissioner Weston Another regular on "The Shadow."

H11.25, B3.7 Professor Quackenbush A Groucho Marx character from the movie *Horsefeathers*.

H12.2, B3.17 quiet ambiguity Couturier points out that the ambiguity stems from Oedipa's ignorance of Pierce's location—"that phone line could have pointed any direction, been any length." Because she does not know all the "coordinates of his discourse," Oedipa cannot accurately assess Pierce's intent (6). This is one of many references to telephone conversations that fail to communicate meaning unequivocally, and part of the novel's preoccupation with messages, signals, noise, information, and transmission.

H12.6, B3.21 to the verge of being forgotten The fact that Pierce is just about to fade from Oedipa's consciousness lends some credence to the suspicion that Oedipa will later develop, that the will is designed "only to harass a one-time mistress" (H178.34).

H12.21, B3.37 the Peninsula That portion of San Mateo County which includes San Francisco at its tip, with the Pacific Ocean to the west and San Francisco Bay to the east.

H12.23, B3.38 "I don't believe in any of it" "This sounds at first like a suburban cliché, but the religious language soon develops in complexity and allusiveness" (Mendelson 124).

H12.29, B4.4 "You're too sensitive" Given Oedipa's later attempt to discover whether she is enough of a "sensitive" to make Nefastis's Maxwell's demon machine work, there is a certain irony to this charge.

H13.7, B4.15 Jack Lemmon American actor nominated for Academy Awards in 1959, 1960, and 1962 for his roles in *Some Like It Hot, The Apartment,* and *Days of Wine and Roses.* Perhaps the association between "lemon" and Mucho's profession is intended, though you would think that the hypersensitive Mucho would try to avoid bringing the word to mind.

H13.17, B4.23 "creampuff" In the realm of used cars, a "creampuff" is a real bargain, a car in splendid condition, and hence, to Mucho, the word seems like a reproach.

H13.20, B4.27 Maybe to excess Olsen takes this sentence, which continues to the middle of the next page, to be imitative of "the complex universe Oedipa inhabits," asserting that its "information density . . . jams the reader's sensibilities" (77).

H13.21, B4.28 people poorer than him The first of many references to those members of contemporary American society who have been passed over, left out of its promise of prosperity and security for all. The "preterite" will figure largely in *Gravity's Rainbow,* and the use of the term to describe the disadvantaged denizens of the world of *Lot 49* derives from the later novel.

H13.22, B4.29 cracker Southern poor white, usually from a rural environment; "probably from their use of whips with a piece of buckskin on the end for cracking" (*New Dictionary of American Slang*).

H13.24, B4.30 motorized, metal extensions of themselves Readers of *V.* will find this image familiar, recalling as it does that novel's preoccupation with the increasing domination of the inanimate over human lives.

H14.1, B4.40 what things had been truly refused The difficulty associated with distinguishing between trash and what has simply been mislaid brings to the reader's attention what will become increasingly important in the novel, namely the idea that the throwaway mentality of contemporary culture may be causing us to lose sight of the potential value of much of our "trash." Seed notices the way in which "rubbish miraculously becomes charged with significance" in this passage (143), and readers familiar with Pynchon's story "Low-lands" may find themselves recalling that the protagonist, Dennis Flange, seems set to begin life over in the heart of a rubbish dump. The WASTE acronym that Oedipa will encounter serves as a further reminder of the importance Pynchon attaches to the concept (H52.13n).

H14.14, B5.12 gray dressing of ash . . . unvarying gray sickness Like the identical days of Oedipa's life, these images of colorless uniformity are suggestive of a culture far gone in the direction of intellectual inertia. They anticipate the ending of *The Courier's Tragedy*, when the world of the play is left to the control of the "colorless administrator," Gennaro (H75.17n).

H14.30, B5.28 Endless, convoluted incest Once again an anticipation of *The Courier's Tragedy*, where incest finds literal expression in the relationship between Francesca and Angelo, and threatens to become convoluted as Angelo schemes to marry Francesca to her son, Pasquale. Here, the figurative usage suggests the kind of closed system that is most susceptible to the inexorable dissipation of energy measured by an increase in the system's entropy. Incest's inwardness, its denial of the need for connection with that which is utterly other than the self, is a useful figure for another, connected aspect of the novel. Oedipa's arrival in San Narciso will initiate a complex set of allusions to the concept of narcissism, which is perhaps foreshadowed here in Mucho's horrified reminiscences.

H14.34, B5.31 KCUF Starting from the fact that western radio station call signs begin with K, Pynchon did not have far to go to arrive at this juvenile joke.

H15.4, B5.35 Krauts in Tiger tanks The German army used Tiger tanks during World War II, notably in the desert of North Africa, where they proved almost invincible.

H15.4, B5.35 gooks with trumpets in the night "Gooks" here refers to North Korean or perhaps Chinese soldiers. The word originated in the Phillipines in 1899 as "a contemptuous term for Filipinos" during the insurrection, and was "probably revived after 1950 by the Korean term *kuk* which is a suffix of nationality" (*New Dictionary of American Slang*). The reference is to the practice during the Korean "conflict" (1950–53) of blowing bugles at night to unnerve United Nations forces. Note the association of the horn with terror or fear.

H15.6, B5.36 whatever it was about the lot We have already learned, of course, what it is about the lot that drove Mucho into the disk-jockey business. That this information is not enough to help Oedipa understand her husband's continued preoccupation with the lot suggests the degree to which she herself has yet to become sensitized to the darker side of the America that is her legacy. The bad dream that haunts Mucho is finally revealed (H144) and it becomes even harder to escape the possibility of some kind of punning connection with the lot that Oedipa will have to come to terms with at the end of the novel—the lot that all the crying is about.

H15.10, B5.40 one day they lose it Mucho will certainly lose it, but not in the sense that Oedipa means here. Rather than shaking the depressing associations that the car lot has for him, Mucho will retreat from them, losing his identity, his grasp on reality, in the process.

H15.15, B6.5 the Top 200 *Billboard* magazine's list of the two hundred most popular records on the market. See also H122.10, where we find Oedipa listening to "songs in the lower stretches of the Top 200, that would never become popular, whose melodies and lyrics would perish as if they had never been sung." The concept of the preterite or passed over is never far from Pynchon's mind, it would seem.

H15.23, B6.13 his fat vortex ring's centre See H25.1n for the possible relevance of this reference to the eye of a storm.

H16.1, B6.24 'fink' Mucho is using the term somewhat loosely, associating Funch's "censorship" with establishment values, and hence with the values of "management," whose interests were served by "finks" or strikebreakers. Of uncertain etymology, the word is linked to "Pink," from "Pinkerton," the name of the agency most readily associated with the practice of violent strikebreaking. Given Mucho's (and Metzger's, and Nefastis's) weakness for "young stuff," this appeal to First Amendment principles has a somewhat hollow ring. Oedipa's dark speculations on statutory rape (H46.2) are not misplaced, it seems.

H16.21, B7.4 another three-in-the-morning phone call The connection with Pierce's "Shadow" call is clear. A further link with

Pierce is established by the indication that Hilarius sounds like Pierce "doing a Gestapo officer." Pierce does voices; Hilarius, we later learn, does faces. By associating Hilarius with Pierce, Pynchon at least opens the possibility that we might think of Pierce as a kind of psychotherapist. After all, it is clear that one motive for Pierce's involvement of Oedipa in the sorting out of his estate could be to help her escape the confines of her tower. Furthermore, although Hilarius will later go completely off the rails, he does offer Oedipa some advice that seems sound enough in the light of her predicament (H138.22).

Couturier comments on the reversal of roles that has taken place in this situation: "In this case, the telephone has apparently pointed in the wrong direction: usually, it is the patient who calls his doctor, not the contrary. . . . The multi-directionality of the telephone line has forced patient and doctor to change parts, as it were: the medium has manipulated those who wanted to use it" (6–7). The reminder that our understanding of the processes of communication must take into account the media which make them possible is a salutary one. *Lot 49* is very much about the transfer of information, and the conflict between rival methods of communication is central.

H16.28, B7.11 her shrink It never becomes clear exactly why Oedipa has need of Hilarius. We are left to infer that she suffers from some nonspecific anxiety, for which Hilarius has prescribed what he claims are tranquilizers.

The drug motif lends weight to Petillon's confident assertion that Hilarius is "obviously Timothy Leary scarcely transmogrified" (127). Apart from that, we can take Hilarius as the joke his name suggests, a cliché of our times, when everyone up-to-date has her or his therapist.

H16.29, B7.11 sounded like Pierce doing a Gestapo officer Given Hilarius's past association with Nazi concentration camp atrocities (H136.33), this is darkly ironic.

H17.8, B7.22 die Brücke Probably a reference to the group of Expressionist painters who gathered in Dresden in 1905 under the name Die Brücke (The Bridge) and were known for their use of drugs as a means of inspiration for their art.

H17.10, B7.24 LSD-25, mescaline, psilocybin Three hallucinogenic drugs with similar effects on the mind. LSD is a synthesized drug, while mescaline and psilocybin are derived from the peyote cactus and from mushrooms, respectively. Hilarius's experiment is comically conceived, but it bears comparison with many of the epidemiological studies conducted in response to the growth of psychotropic drug use in the sixties.

H17.12, B7.26 The bridge inward Given Oedipa's sense of buffered isolation, and the images of solipsistic enclosure that will proliferate throughout the novel, we are ready to sympathize with her mistrustfulness of Hilarius's efforts to draw her into his research project. We will later see Mucho groping "further and further into the rooms and endless rooms of the elaborate candy house of himself" (H153.3n) after joining Hilarius's program.

H17.17, B7.31 the well-known portrait of Uncle The portrait's association with post offices is surely not coincidental. The unhealthy gleam and the sunken cheeks of this seemingly diseased icon of the state are linked by association with the mail system that the state controls. Those who would argue that the Tristero's opposition to the state monopoly represents a possible liberation might well see grist for their mill in this juxtaposition.

H17.21, B7.35 afraid of all he might answer Oedipa's fearfulness, linked as it is with the somewhat nightmarish image of Uncle Sam, is an early indication of her tendency to think in ways that might be construed as paranoid. Just what it is that Hilarius could tell her that she would not want to hear is not at all clear.

H17.25, B7.39 "Don't describe it" At this point, it seems that Hilarius is simply attempting to avoid a therapy session—shirking his professional responsibilities. Later, Hilarius will tell Oedipa to "cherish" her fantasies, to protect them from the Freudians and the pharmacists alike (H138.22). His advice here is possibly similarly motivated.

H17.33, B8.7 Literally damned This seems somewhat melodramatic on Oedipa's part at this early stage. Given what happens to Mucho under Hilarius's ministrations, however, we might revise our opinion.

H18.10, B8.17 Rorschach blot   Named after the Swiss psychiatrist Hermann Rorschach (1884–1922). Subjects are asked to "read" symmetrical ink blots. "The Rorschach test is based on the human tendency to project interpretations and feelings onto ambiguous stimuli" (*Encyclopedia Britannica*). This definition is particularly apt in the light of Oedipa's later efforts to interpret the ambiguous clues that begin to proliferate around her.

H18.11, B8.18 TAT picture   The Thematic Aperception Test developed in 1938 by H. A. Murray requires the subject to interpret a picture by telling a story about what has led up to the particular scene, what is happening in the scene, and what is likely to happen in the future.

H18.14, B8.27 "Fu-Manchu"   The creation of Sax Rohmer (Arthur Henry Ward), Fu-Manchu first saw light in 1911 along with his Holmes-like adversary, Dennis Nayland Smith. Fu-Manchu was said to be "evil incarnate" and, according to Rohmer, was "the embodiment of the Yellow Peril."

H18.25, B8.32 the Perry Mason television program   The show starred Raymond Burr as an inordinately successful lawyer. From September 1957 to September 1966, CBS aired 271 episodes.

H18.27, B8.34 a fierce ambivalence   Roseman's feelings about Perry Mason are an anticipation of our introduction to Metzger, the actor-turned-lawyer whose life becomes the basis of a TV series in which he is played by a lawyer-turned-actor (H33).

H19.4, B9.3 "You didn't use to look guilty"   Roseman's obsession with Perry Mason is clearly associated with complete derangement —the photographer who thinks he is a volleyball. That Oedipa regards Roseman's guilty look as a good sign indicates her own sense of the inappropriateness of his behavior. If he is looking guilty, he must be getting "better." As her horizons widen during the course of her quest, however, Oedipa will become more tolerant of deviance from a norm that increasingly seems constrictive. She does not sit in judgment on the behavior of the people she encounters during her nighttime journey through the streets of San Francisco.

H19.25, B9.22 So, insulated   Oedipa will attempt a similar degree of insulation during her next encounter with a lawyer. With Metz-ger, however, there occurs a gradual stripping away of the layers (H41.11).

H19.29, B9.26   That shut him up.   Roseman wants intimacy with-out commitment. This rather shopworn exchange anticipates the failure of love that leaves Oedipa utterly on her own by the end of the novel. As we will see, some critics regard the dissolution of Oedipa's relationships with men as a positive factor in her progress toward self-discovery (H152.32n).

H20.10, B9.40   revelations   The concept of revelation will play a key part in the novel. Its religious overtones have been noted by a number of critics: it "suggests the centrality of religion in Oedipa's quest" (Nicholson 94); it "opens up the possibility of a religious dimension to the novel" (Tanner, "Crying" 180).

H20.10, B9.40   Hardly about . . . herself   Notwithstanding the nar-rator's claim here, several critics argue that what Oedipa learns is very much about herself. Davidson writes of the "feminist per-ceptions" that Oedipa develops and claims that she undergoes a "dawning awareness" (42). Watson argues that Oedipa's whole quest is one of self-discovery, and he concludes that "Oedipa is shut into the auction hall to confront herself" (70). We have already noted Kolodny and Peters's insistence that Oedipa experiences "a change of consciousness" (82).

H20.11, B10.1   about what had remained   Tanner in particular takes note of the strangeness of this description: "That sense of some-thing that had somehow remained and yet stayed away . . . suggests strange states of mind, odd intimations of something between presence and absence, a sense of something, an image, a picture, a plot that is not quite visibly *there* but not quite visibly *not* there either. Such strange sensations, which seem to take place at the very interface between meaning and nonmeaning, will occur to Oedipa increasingly" ("Crying" 180).

One might argue that this "revelation" is strongly suggestive of the novel's focus on Oedipa's self-discovery. "What had remained," we could suppose, refers to the residue of her relationship with Pierce, a net addition to the insight that she had already arrived at in Mexico City (and Mazatlán?), but one of which she is not conscious until the "job of sorting it all out" brings it to the surface. She has been unable to gain access to this residue of meaning precisely because of the "buffering, insulation" that has cocooned her; it has "stayed away" until Metzger's letter begins the process of stripping away the layers of insulation.

H20.16, B10.6 the curious, Rapunzel-like role Schaub notes the conflict between the idea that Oedipa has "conned herself" into the role of Rapunzel and the notion that she is "magically" held prisoner. "The tower quickly establishes an ambiguity which never resolves, for we are never sure whether it is an image of solipsism or one of imprisonment by forces outside Oedipa" (31). Other critics seem less inclined to settle for uncertainty. Mendelson, for example, insists that the tower "is not a product of the self, but one of the conditions of this world" (136), while Davidson suggests what those conditions might be: "For one so long imprisoned, solutions which depend on independent action are not readily discernible. Predictably, such a 'captive maiden,' in typical *heroine* fashion, clings to the hope that some gallant rescuer will save her from a life that is, she knows, unsatisfactory" (44). At the same time, when Rapunzel's prison is re-envisioned very shortly as the tower in the Varo painting, the suggestion of solipsistic enclosure is too strong to be ignored (H21).

H20.23, B10.13 sinister sorcery Deriving, presumably, from the same source as the magic that holds Oedipa prisoner. The alliteration seems deliberately contrived for comic effect.

The allegory of the captive princess who cannot be rescued by conventional means serves to prepare the reader for Oedipa's increasing estrangement from the predictability of her life in Kinneret. As a parallel to Pynchon's princess in the tower, see Donald Barthelme's *Snow White*, in which the beleaguered Snow White hangs her ebony hair from the window of her apartment, only to find that no one responds to her "hair initiative."

H20.25, B10.14 on his ass The broad comedy of Pierce's failure is tinged with bitterness almost immediately when Oedipa learns the lesson of the Varo painting (H21.24n).

H20.26, B10.15   credit cards for a shim   We are probably well accustomed by now to the image on film and television of the intrepid investigator or evil villain opening doors with a credit card. I am not aware, however, of that image having been exploited for its painfully obvious symbolic value, as it is here. "True guile" is indication enough of Oedipa's sense of the indirectness of the capitalist approach to love implicit in Pierce's means of entry to her tower.

H21.1, B10.21   Remedios Varo   Kaplan informs us that Maria de Los Remedios Varo y Uranga was born on December 16, 1908 (not 1913, as has been assumed), in Angles, north of Barcelona, in the province of Catalonia (7). According to Cowart, she felt stifled by the constraints of her conventional existence but felt obliged nonetheless to conform. "Varo continued to embroider the traditional world-mantle until the Spanish civil war gave her an excuse to leave the country and go to Paris. There she met her own knight of deliverance, the surrealist poet, Benjamin Peret, with whom she emigrated to Mexico" (22).

H21.1, B10.22   the central painting of a triptych   Reproductions of the painting appear in a number of readily available sources. Kaplan's color plates offer the best look, but monochrome versions appear in Colville and Grace, among others. Pynchon may well have seen this triptych in August 1964 at an exhibition of 124 of Varo's paintings at the Palacio de Bellas Artes in Mexico City. Cowart has written at some length about the Varo triptych: "the castle is seen in the left panel, *Hacia La Torre*; in the foreground is a group of uniformly dressed girls, all but one of whom appear mesmerized, who are made to embroider in the tower of the central panel. The central panel . . . contains more than Oedipa notices: in one of the folds of the extruded tapestry—out in the world, that is—lurks a tiny, shadowy figure, the lover of the unmesmerized girl. She, perhaps realizing that if all reality is embroidered then the tower itself must be embroidered, is engaged in embroidering her way out of the tower by means of a *trampa* (Varo's word; it means 'trick' or 'trapdoor') in order to escape to her lover. She is successful, for they appear together in the right panel, *La Huida* [The Escape], presumably voyaging toward new realities" (22–23).

The "trampa" to which Cowart refers is reproduced as a detail in Kaplan's book (21); it is an inverted depiction of a lovers' tryst, presumably anticipating, as Cowart suggests, the meeting and escape of the girl and her lover. We may have some difficulty associating this putative outcome with Oedipa, whose lovers all abandon her and who is never sure whether she is "voyaging toward new realities" or retreating into paranoia.

The description of the tower and the embroidering girls becomes the basis for further differences of opinion concerning the tower's symbolic significance. Davidson finally associates the tower with the men who exploit and abandon Oedipa: "She can escape from the tower only after she has become free of these men" (45). Hite, on the other hand, clearly sees the tower as indicative of Oedipa's self-enclosure: "Oedipa, confronted by a vision of her own world as the product of her own solipsistic 'embroidering,' realizes that in this case there can be no escape" (81). In this view Hite is joined by Tanner, at least at one stage of his discussion. He claims that the painting "is of course a lyrical reflection of Oedipa's own embroidery work, those self-spun versions of reality with which she tries to fill the void" ("V." 41). However, Tanner goes on to acknowledge the external nature of the magic that holds Oedipa prisoner, thus aligning himself more with someone like Seed, for whom Oedipa's confrontation with the painting is a salutary experience: "It is a key moment for Oedipa when she sees the painting and she is moved to tears by the realization that her self-image [as Rapunzel] was fanciful and that she is held in place by 'magic'" (139–40). Seed goes on to attribute a significance to the painting that "goes beyond what Oedipa perceives so that it makes reference to broader aspects of the novel. The tower, for instance, is surrounded by thin clouds which find alternative expression in California's smog-haze. The four [actually, there seem to be six] girls are presided over by a sinister hooded figure in black who looks forward to the mysterious figures in the play. By a strange coincidence in the background of the tower a figure (also in black) is playing a long instrument which slightly resembles a kind of horn" (140).

In keeping with another very common critical approach to the novel as a whole, which emphasizes the self-reflexive characteristics of many of the novel's motifs, Hall draws attention to the fact that the hooded figure is holding a book ("the controlling Word") and is thus the personification of the logocentrism that keeps the girls under its "imprisoning spell" (70).

H21.10, B10.30 perverse Why? What is perverse about Oedipa's being moved to tears by a painting that seems to capture the spirit of her own imprisonment?

H21.17, B10.36 see the world refracted through those tears Oedipa is never really able to shake the effect of those tears. She finds herself at the end of the novel still unable to determine whether she has been liberated from the tower by Pierce's legacy or simply more securely confined.

H21.24, B11.3 there'd been no escape Oedipa's realization seems to confirm the reading of the painting that emphasizes its solipsistic implications. She recognizes here that her relationship with Pierce is fabricated, woven together out of hopes generated by a process of socialization, rather than developed out of some genuine human connectedness. Like Barthelme's Snow White, Oedipa has clung to the notion that someday her prince will come, only to discover that princeliness as a concept does not correspond to anything objectively real in the world outside the self.

H21.29, B11.7 magic, anonymous and malignant By this stage we may be ready to see a degree of complementarity in the apparently conflicting notions of solipsism and magic. The individual is forced into the acceptance of her Rapunzel-like role by the "magic" of acculturation, which is certainly anonymous and can undoubtedly be malignant in its effects. That this magic is "formless" adds to its threat, given our innate desire to project form on the universe we inhabit. "Shall I project a world?" Oedipa will later ask herself (H82.11n).

H21.31, B11.10 female cunning A concept that may not have seemed problematic when the novel was first published. I am not sure that today's readers are going to be able to read this without at least a momentary pause for reflection. Just what is "female cunning" anyway?

H22.1, B11.11   count its lines of force   Seed finds grounds for optimism about Oedipa's future in this: "Oedipa has significantly exchanged a metaphor of confinement for one of openness (fields of force) which looks forward to her receptivity towards insights later in the novel. . . . If it is doubt she feels [about external reality], it is a liberating doubt and the first step in Oedipa's sloughing off of her suburban attitudes" (140).

H22.2, B11.12   fall back on superstition   In a sense we have watched Oedipa run through this list already. She speaks the name of God, implicitly identifies with the frail girls embroidering in the tower, accuses herself of being "so sick" and attends group therapy sessions, and marries the disk jockey Mucho Maas. Having exhausted these possibilities, then, she is left with the "what else?" with which the first chapter concludes. The quest on which Oedipa is about to embark is thus a quest in search of the answer to this question. According to Davidson: "The answer, the something else, must be one's self. Oedipa at last becomes her own knight of deliverance" (45).

Johnston notes that the quadruple choice outlined here "mirrors symmetrically the set of possibilities she is left with at the novel's end" (53).

◌◁]] Chapter 2

H23.3, B12.3   "I Want to Kiss Your Feet"   The song that Mucho is whistling contains in its title an allusion to the legend of Saint Narcissus, third century bishop of Jerusalem. Oedipa will learn during the performance of *The Courier's Tragedy* of the death of the good Duke of Faggio as a result of his practice of kissing the feet in a picture of the saint (H65.21n). This is one of many embedded pointers to the novel's preoccupation with the concept of narcissism.

Cooper sees in such internal allusiveness a version for the reader of Oedipa's sense that a pattern is revealing itself just beyond her capacity to grasp it. "The book delivers not revelation but rather the *mood* of revelation, of the dawning perception that '*everything is connected*, everything in the Creation,' woven into a plot that could be miraculous or malign depending on the perceiver who partially constructs it" (177).

Note that the song echoes the Beatles hit "I Want to Hold Your Hand," which was number four on the American charts in April 1964.

H23.4, B12.3   Sick Dick and the Volkswagens   Part, no doubt, of the "British Invasion" that began with the appearance of the Beatles on the "Ed Sullivan Show" in 1964. The name serves a dual purpose, linking the new sound of the invading Brits to the fifties Doo-wop of "car" groups such as the Jaguars, the Eldorados, the Cadillacs, and the Edsels. On the British side, the name is reminiscent of such groups as Gerry and the Pacemakers, Wayne Fontana and the Mindbenders, Freddy and the Dreamers, Eric Burdon and the Animals, Simon Dupree and the Big Sound, etc.

Mac Adam (565) connects "Sick Dick" with Richard Wharfinger, author of *The Courier's Tragedy*, that "ill, ill Jacobean revenge play" (H63.21).

H23.7, B12.6   San Narciso   As Palmeri points out, the name of the city that Pierce has created invokes a number of subtexts, "late classical, Christian and Freudian" (985). Ovid's account of the story of Narcissus and Echo, the church historian Eusebius's retelling of the miracles associated with Saint Narcissus, and Freud's essay "On Narcissism" offer "competing paradigms" within or against which Pynchon's own manipulation of symbolic possibilities can be read (987).

Schaub and Abernethy add Marshall McLuhan to Ovid in their analyses of Pynchon's use of the Narcissus myth. Both quote McLuhan's association of the word "narcissus" with "narcosis," or numbness. "The youth Narcissus mistook his own reflection in the water for another person. This extension of himself by mirror numbed his perceptions until he became the servomechanism of his own extended or repeated image. The nymph Echo tried to win his love with fragments of his own speech, but in vain. He was numb. He had adapted to his extension of himself and had become a closed system" (McLuhan in Abernethy 28). Abernethy's concern is with the contribution this image of enclosure makes to the novel's vision of entropic decline. Note the linking of narcissism and closed systems that has already been hinted at in Mucho's feelings about the "convoluted incest" of the car lot. Schaub's associations are perhaps more direct: "Pynchon's direct evocation of the Narcissus myth is a clear statement that Pierce's estate and what it represents are a culture in love with a dream-image of itself" (25).

Watson argues that Pynchon invokes the myth in order to indicate the dual nature of Oedipa's perceptions: "Oedipa fears that, if she believes in the Tristero, she will prove to be Narcissus, mistaking the creations of her own confused perceptions for external reality. But if she refuses to believe in it, she risks discovering that it is a version of Echo, a real warning from an all-too-real creature which she . . . fails to heed" (70).

H24.3, B12.14   a grouping of concepts   "The city is not real; it is textual: everything has been meticulously planned, projected, in advance. The city existed on paper before it found its way onto an actual tract of land and eventually onto a map of California" (Couturier 15). According to Nicholson, this is what "the open frontier has become . . . under the control of moguls like Pierce Inverarity" (98).

H24.11, B13.4   any vital difference   At this stage of her quest, Oedipa is unable to see what might separate San Narciso from the rest of the state(s). As she moves deeper and deeper into the world of Pierce's legacy America, however, Oedipa must begin to perceive a difference, for we will learn toward the end of the novel that San Narciso gives up its "residue of uniqueness for her . . . [and is] assumed back into the American continuity of crust and mantle" (H177.29).

H24.14, B13.7   Nothing was happening.   From the beginning, San Narciso is portrayed as a community in which life is stagnant, in which intellectual exchange has ceased to take place. The portrayal is entirely consistent with the novel's development of images associated with entropy.

H24.25, B13.17   a hieroglyphic sense of concealed meaning   The concept of hidden meaning that must be teased out is of course central to the novel. That the concealment of meaning is conceived of in terms of hieroglyphs perhaps reflects more of Pynchon's demonstrable interest in the esoterica of priestly knowledge than Oedipa's inherent openness to experience of a specifically religious kind. Nevertheless, the word does convey the sense of sacred meaning and thus connects with the frequent use of the word "revelation" throughout the novel.

H24.29, B13.20   a revelation also trembled   The issue of whether the messages that Oedipa begins to receive emanate from some sacred source or whether they are purely secular in nature is raised with a vengeance by this passage. Mendelson acknowledges that we cannot be absolutely sure at this point, but he argues backward from subsequent, less ambiguous invocations of the sacred and thus seems inclined to read this potential revelation as being sacred in nature (118). Tanner grants that "there is the possibility of some kind of religious communication," but also wonders whether the something that is being revealed remains "on a sinister secular level, or on a more sacred plane" ("Crying" 181). Seed seems to favor a more secular interpretation: "The repeated use of the term 'revelation' could . . . be taken in a non-transcendental sense, to refer to her discovery of a California (and hence an America) which she did not know existed" (134).

H24.33, B13.24   an odd, religious instant   This seems unequivocal in its evocation of the sacred. Note, however, that on the very next page, the experience is called into question.

Petillon notes that "the instant is not odd because religious, but religious because odd" (141).

H24.33, B13.25   some other frequency   This moment is potentially religious in part because of Oedipa's sense that the message she is not quite able to receive is being transmitted from somewhere beyond the confines of normal experience. The idea of revelation, so frequently and so tantalizingly repeated in the novel, is very much connected with this possible intrusion of one world into another (see, particularly, H120.7n—Oedipa's conversation with Jesús Arrabal).

H25.1–4, B13.25–27 some whirlwind ... She thought of Mucho Perhaps she is in part moved to think of Mucho by a process of association. She has earlier (H15.22) envisaged him "smiling out of his fat vortex ring's center," emanating a deceptive air of calmness. Here, however, she places Mucho, as she places herself, outside the center, away from the sacred gestures/meanings that are being generated in some inaccessible other place. For the time being, at least, she associates herself with Mucho's inability to believe, but with a sense of sadness that gives promise of some degree of change.

H25.9, B13.32 chrism, censer, chalice Used in various Christian ceremonies, these are, respectively, a consecrated mixture of oil and balsam, an incense vessel, and a cup that holds the wine during Communion services.

Madsen sees the image of Oedipa looking through the glass at Mucho the "priest" as indicative of "her sense of exclusion from a circumscribed field of discourse" (56).

H25.17, B13.39 the "religious instant" As Mendelson points out, "the narrator dismisses Oedipa's experience by placing it in distancing quotation marks" (118). Since the narrative voice seems so consistently close to Oedipa's, we can surely assume that the "whatever it might've been" that adds to our sense of the dismissiveness here is more or less a direct quote. Oedipa is not prepared at this moment to grant transcendental standing to any aspect of her experience.

H25.25, B14.7 It seemed unnatural. In summarizing what he takes to be the "normative" reading of the novel, David Bennett alludes to San Narciso as "a world of artifice in which nothing is gratuitous or natural, everything implicit with some intention or design" (34). While Oedipa does not explicitly derive any concrete meaning from the numbers, she does "read" them as out of the ordinary and thus as potentially significant. As her quest proceeds, of course, she will become increasingly likely to interpret such aberrations as clues to the "design" of the Tristero.

H25.30, B14.12   YOYODYNE   "A company with factories scattered careless about the country and more government contracts than it really knew what to do with" (*V.* 225) (see H83.29n for more on this). We find Stencil touring a Yoyodyne plant on Long Island in *V.*, and Benny Profane is employed briefly by Anthroresearch Associates, a subsidiary of Yoyodyne. Profane's job is to keep an eye on SHOCK and SHROUD, two research dummies that are disturbingly accurate simulacra of human beings.

Abernethy ties the company to the idea of entropy that is beginning to become important in the novel: "Since Yoyodyne is a military research and development laboratory, designed to react to stimuli from other 'R & D' oufits, both foreign and domestic, its products are oriented toward the meaningless cycle of producing weapons to counter other weapons which, in turn, will themselves have to be countered. It is a closed system. The image of the Yoyo fits: it represents energy expended in a cycle of activity which, for all its apparent dynamism, is essentially meaningless mechanical repetition" (27–28).

Tyson attaches some significance to the fact that the plant buildings are painted pink, suggesting that this "empty sign of the usual mark of the patriarchal girl-child" serves to disguise Yoyodyne's "ominous function" (9). The two phallic, "sixty-foot missiles" on either side of the factory gate would seem to advertise, rather than conceal, however.

H26.5, B14.19   founding father   As the implications of Oedipa's involvement in the affairs of Pierce Inverarity broaden to suggest that somehow America itself is the legacy he has bequeathed her, this association of Pierce with the history of the nation assumes a retrospective significance, and the irony of the fact that the "founding" takes place in part through backroom deals takes on a bitter tone.

H26.10, B14.24   silence and paralysis   Schaub notes the lack of movement and associates it with the numbness implicit in McLuhan's reading of the Narcissus myth (26). Oedipa's fanciful vision of the road as a hypodermic needle later in the same paragraph legitimizes this association through the link it creates with the cognate "narcotic." The paralysis is also congruent, of course, with the stagnation of highly entropic systems.

H26.15, B14.28 it wasn't A lesson Oedipa will learn later in the novel (H108.27n), when she finds that the "freeway madness" is preferable to the silence and calm of San Narciso.

H26.25, B14.38 a white blossom Palmeri speculates that the flower may be *Narcissus poetica* (986).

H26.27, B14.39 Echo Courts The allusion to the Narcissus myth is broad and unmistakable. The nymph on the sign is a grotesque parody of Ovid's pining nymph. The resemblance to Oedipa is suggestive, tempting us to read Oedipa as Echo. Berressem takes note of this resemblance, arguing that it "implies that . . . Oedipa is in love with the narcissistic culture of which she herself is so much a part," and that "Oedipa's language is never her own but consists of cultural fragments she merely reflects" (95).

For Tyson, the sign is "the empty sign of empty sex, the perfect wet dream of the existentially disengaged" (9).

H27.9, B15.13 swimming pool Both Palmeri (986) and Watson (70) see the swimming pool as equivalent to the pool in which Narcissus sees his fatal reflection.

H27.15, B15.28 a Beatle haircut By the prevailing standards of the day the Beatles wore their hair daringly long, though the sculpted style was far from the unkempt "Jesus" look that was soon to become fashionable.

H27.15, B15.29 a lapelless, cuffless, one-button mohair suit The "uniform" made popular by the Beatles.

H27.25, B15.28 Frug . . . Swim Two of the many short-lived dance styles of the early sixties.

H28.6, B16.1 the Payola Kid Miles is referring to the practice of paying radio disk jockeys to give more air time to particular recordings. A congressional probe into the practice in 1960 had resulted in the dismissal of a number of DJs.

H28.14, B16.9 four bits A "bit" originally referred to one of the "small silver coins forming fractions of the Spanish dollar" (*OED*).

In its most recent manifestation, the (nonexistent) bit has been valued at 12½ cents, so "four bits" is 50 cents.

H28.17, B16.12 It had to be an actor. Couturier claims that "reality has been so transformed by the cinema and television, by the many techniques of simulation, that Oedipa can't trust her eyes" (8). However, the fact is that Metzger *has been* an actor, so Oedipa's mildly paranoid response to his impossible good looks is not altogether out of line, as she very soon realizes.

H28.25, B16.20 smuggled last year into California An inquiry sent to the California Department of Food and Agriculture elicited the following response from the department's legal representative: "I've served as Department Counsel for this Department since 1961 and I am unaware that it was ever necessary to 'smuggle' French wine into California. I have found no statute or ordinance imposing import restrictions or tariffs relevant to this matter." Perhaps Metzger has simply exceeded his wine and liquor allowance on a trip to Mexico.

H28.31, B16.25 *Bonanza* The television western chronicling the adventures of the Cartwright family on their ranch, the Ponderosa. This show debuted in September 1959 and ran for 440 episodes until January 1973.

H29.10, B16.36 really out to kasher me "Kasher" is an alternative form of "kosher," which means to make fit according to Jewish dietary laws. In this case, Metzger is referring to the draining of blood from slaughtered animals and thus, by a stretch, to his mother's "draining" his manhood. No doubt Pynchon was well aware of the irony of Metzger's name here ("metzger" means "butcher").

H29.22, B17.6 aware it was all words Oedipa assumes, with some justification, that Metzger's fears about his sexual identity are a kind of come-on. Given his later defection with a fifteen-year-old, however, there may be more to it than that.

H29.31, B17.25 a child of indeterminate sex Reminiscent of other child stars of the past—among them Freddy Bartholomew in his role as the ringleted and knickerclad Little Lord Fauntleroy.

H30.11, B17.27 "About you and your mother." Oedipa, who will turn out to be "a whiz at pursuing strange words in Jacobean texts" (H104.19), reveals a taste for word games here. Although no etymological link can be forged between "kashered" and "cashiered," the two have a loose, punning congruence that affords Oedipa an opportunity to express a playful incredulity at what she perhaps still takes to be Metzger's attempt to put the moves on her. Metzger evidently does not get the joke.

H30.15, B17.31   Gallipoli   The Gallipoli Peninsula in southwestern Turkey separates the Aegean Sea from the Dardanelles, a channel leading from the Aegean into the Sea of Marmara and north to Istanbul. This was the site of a yearlong military campaign, from February 1915 to January 1916, during which British, Australian, and New Zealand forces attempted to launch an invasion of Turkey intended to knock Turkey out of World War I and open up supply routes to Russia. Poor timing on the part of British commanders resulted in the failure of the campaign.

H30.25, B18.1   phony-Dodecanese process footage   Process footage is film projected onto a screen to form the backdrop for live action by the actors. Here the attempt is to create the impression that the movie's action is taking place on an island in the Aegean.

H31.8, B18.16   Either he made up the whole thing   A kind of warm-up for Oedipa's later doubts about the Tristero. She will come to wonder whether Pierce might have fabricated its existence "as a pure conspiracy against someone he loved," or whether in fact he might have discovered the existence of the Tristero and "encrypted" enough of it in his will to be sure she would find it (H179.4). It is interesting to note that even at this early stage Oedipa is alert to the possibility of elaborate plotting.

Unlike the binary oppositions of her later dilemma, however, both possibilities here point in the same direction; whether Metzger made up the whole Baby Igor scenario or simply arranged a screening of the movie, his object, Oedipa supposes, is the same.

H31.14, B18.22   Fangoso Lagoons   "Fangoso" means "muddy" or "slimy" in Italian.

"Fangoso Lagoons must not be an ordinary place in California; it is supposed to look different. One could almost speak of an intertextual place, each item pointing towards an idealized representation of another country, towards another text. . . . [It is a place] whose chief function is to bolster the shaky reality of the world outside" (Couturier 15).

H31.16, B18.24 "One of Inverarity's interests" Seed argues that "one of Metzger's main roles in the novel is to alert Oedipa to Inverarity as a force" (118).

H31.28, B18.36 some promise of hierophany Once again the possibility of sacred meanings is adumbrated. Mendelson traces the word "hierophany" to Mircea Eliade's *The Sacred and the Profane*: "Man becomes aware of the sacred because it manifests itself, shows itself, as something wholly different from the profane. To designate the *act of manifestation* of the sacred, we have proposed the term *hierophany*. It is a fitting term because it does not imply anything further; it expresses no more than is implicit in its etymological content, *i.e.*, that *something sacred shows itself to us*. . . . From the most elementary hierophany . . . to the supreme hierophany . . . there is no solution of continuity. In each case we are confronted by the same mysterious act—the manifestation of something of a wholly different order, a reality that does not belong to our world, in objects that are an integral part of our natural 'profane' world" (122). The stress on difference is of key importance, for it ties hierophany to revelation, the term used most frequently in the novel to suggest the possibility of meanings other than those we are accustomed to.

H31.29, B18.37 private access to the water, Book of the Dead It is hard to be certain of the chain of associations that Oedipa is forging here, though it seems to be based on a combination of visual and linguistic stimuli. The grid pattern of the lagoon development reminds her of the streets of San Narciso, which she had felt contained "a hieroglyphic sense of concealed meaning" (H24.25n). The common prefix links "hieroglyphic" with "hierophany," and the two together allow the association of the canals with the Egyptian *Book of the Dead*, portions of which are written in "hieratic" script. The sixth division of the Egyptian netherworld, the realm of Osiris, is said to be a country of fields intersected with canals, to which only the worthy gain access after their trial in the Hall of the Two Truths. "Private," with its attendant implication of wealth and privilege, may be connected for Oedipa with the fact that the more elaborate funeral practices of early Egypt were confined to the families of the most powerful members of society. "Access to the water" could thus be linked either to the canals of Osiris's bucolic paradise or more literally to the Nile, across which the bodies of the privileged dead would be transported for ceremonial burial.

It is possible, though less easily accounted for, that Oedipa is thinking of the *Tibetan Book of the Dead*, the *Bardo Thodrol Chenmo*, a book that had become increasingly popular as American counterculture fascination with Buddhism grew. Critics have noted that Tibetan beliefs include the notion that the soul undergoes a forty-nine-day period of "becoming" after death. While it could be argued that Oedipa is in a transitional stage of her life, a kind of rebirth, the numerological coincidence (which in any case is not specifically invoked at this moment) is probably not enough to outweigh the clear associations with Egyptian motifs.

H32.9, B19.9   the Narrows . . . the Kephez minefields   The Turks had strung mines across the narrowest part of the straits to inhibit the passage of warships into the Sea of Marmara. Submarines, which could go beneath the mines, were the only means of access to the sea. These minefields had been instrumental at the very beginning of the campaign in dissuading the British from pursuing the military advantage they had gained by a naval bombardment of Turkish forts.

H32.11, B19.10   this gigantic net   Metzger's account appears to be more or less accurate, with the exception of his claim that "all" the British subs used the gate. Moorhead asserts that "unless the subs were lucky enough to strike [the gate] their only way of getting through the wire was to ram it at full speed underwater and hope for the best." Moorhead also notes that "up to the last . . . the passage through the Narrows remained an ordeal of the most frightening kind" (215).

H32.29, B19.26   "Wasn't I there?"   The conflation of the real and the fictional here is reminiscent of Roseman's uncertain attitude toward Perry Mason, a foretaste of the novel's strategic blurring of distinctions between the historically verifiable and the possibly contrived.

H33.13, B20.3 **"this extended capacity for convolution"** I have already noted the connection with Roseman's obsession with Perry Mason (H18.27n). Another retrospective link is surely with Mucho's vision of the "endless, convoluted incest" of the car lot (H14.30n).

H33.25, B20.14 **"it can be repeated endlessly"** Abernethy, citing Metzger as an example of a narcissistic closed system of a McLuhanesque kind, suggests that Metzger's "sense of the value of this reproduction of himself as a means of 'preserving' his identity is false. As Wiener says, 'The idea that information can be stored in a changing world without an overwhelming depreciation in its value is false' " (29). We may find ourselves tempted to make the same observation when Oedipa speculates later in the novel on the possibility that Pierce may have fabricated the Tristero as a means of preserving his identity beyond death.

H33.26, B20.16 **"You're in trouble"** Just what kind of trouble is Metzger in? Is this simply a glib response to the convolutions of Metzger's account, or does Oedipa sense in the permutations that he runs through a genuine loss of stable identity?

H34.30, B21.11 **Feeling the words had been conned out of her.** Oedipa is of course correct in her prediction, but she feels uneasy because she is betting on an outcome that violates the norms of the Hollywood movie genre, norms that she would instinctively favor under other circumstances. Hall argues that Pynchon is deliberately undermining genre as a guide to interpretation (67).

H34.30, B21.12 **"Another bottle tonight would put you to sleep"** Remember that Oedipa gets at least tipsy on the kirsch in the fondue. Another bottle tonight would probably kill her.

H35.13, B21.25 **kissing its palm** Nicholson sees this as part of the novel's "pentecostal imagery of tongues," noting that Metzger is "tonguing her fate literally, and affecting her fate crucially" (94–95).

H35.28, B21.39 **irrepressibly comic** Whose judgment is this? Are we really expected to think of Metzger as a charming clown whose mission in life is to loosen up the uptight Oedipa? Or is this a tongue-in-cheek epithet delivered as if by Oedipa herself and thus intended to maintain some distance from Metzger? Maybe the fact that she is angry would incline us to the latter view.

H36.6, B22.8 "Strip Botticelli" The game that Metzger proposes is more like the simple Twenty Questions than Botticelli, in which the questioner has to earn the right to ask direct questions by first stumping her opponent with indirect ones. See the *Oxford Guide to Word Games* for a full description.

Johnston, arguing that sexual seduction may be seen as a parody of revelation, suggests that the game, "which, not incidentally, requires the gradual revelation of the flesh in accordance with the reading and interpretation of signs or 'clues' in a Hollywood film—strongly indicates that the 'revelation in progress all around her' may also be a seduction" (50). Johnston argues that Metzger's conversation with Pierce, apparently about Oedipa's sexual availability (H43.17), is further evidence for this claim.

Newman sees the game as "a metaphor for the unmasking quest pattern of the book" (78).

H36.10, B22.12 the "River Clyde" "Accordingly at 5 a.m. in the uncertain first light of the morning the battleship *Albion* opened up a tremendous bombardment on the village and the cove. There was no reply from the shore. After an hour it was judged that the Turks there must be either demoralized or dead, and the *River Clyde* with her two thousand men on board was ordered to the shore. . . . Thus it was in broad daylight and on the calmest of seas that the soldiers approached the shore. An unnatural stillness had succeeded the barrage. . . . At 6.22 a.m. the *River Clyde* grounded her bows without a tremor just below the fortress and the first of the boats was within a few yards of the shore.

"In that instant the Turkish rifle fire broke out. . . . Air Commodore Samson came flying over Sedd-el-Bahr . . . and looking down saw that the calm sea was 'absolutely red with blood' for a distance of fifty yards from the shore" (Moorhead 141–43).

H36.20, B22.21 began putting on as much as she could "In doing so she becomes a grotesque image of an insanely eclectic culture which 'over-dresses' itself with bits and pieces of fabrics and fabrications taken from anywhere" (Tanner, "Crying" 178). "She is not thinking about her husband any more, but trying to protect herself against sexual aggression. She is attracted to this actor/lawyer, but at the same time she is afraid of sex" (Couturier 23).

H36.26, B22.27   old Orlon muu-muu   This sounds like an odd garment for Oedipa to have packed for her trip south. Orlon is an acrylic fiber usually used to emulate cashmere and thus is hardly the kind of yarn that a muu-muu (a loose-fitting, brightly colored garment usually associated with Hawaii) would be made of.

H37.1, B22.35   propelling the can swiftly about the bathroom   "In the spray can caroming off the walls of the motel bathroom we have both an image of entropy—a region of fast molecules with the can exhausting itself within the the confines of the bathroom—and an image of human life threatened, albeit comically, by the systems it has created" (Schaub 26).

Slade notes that the can duplicates James Prescott Joule's experiments with the expansion of gases, and cites Henry Adams in *The Education:* "The kinetic theory of gas is an assertion of ultimate chaos" (Slade 131).

"The bomb of hair-spray that shatters Oedipa's bathroom mirror announces the impending blitz of her self-satisfaction and confidence, and the development in her of a receptivity to a true otherness" (Nohrnberg 152).

According to Couturier, the spray can is "phallic" and is "ejaculating all around the room, threatening to upset everything" (25).

H37.19, B23.12   the complex web of its travel   Oedipa has a conventional faith in the ultimate determinability of phenomena, a faith that she does not appear to abandon. A common reading of Oedipa's predicament at the end of the novel maintains that she is anxiously awaiting the evidence that will resolve her doubts and enable her to account fully and unambiguously for the complex mass of data that she has accumulated.

Of course, there are those who would argue to the contrary—see, for example, Nicholson, who claims that Oedipa finally realizes that "a more anarchic sense of her world's possibilities is enabling. It is in this arduously achieved Keatsian state of uncertainty that Oedipa tremulously awaits 'the crying of lot 49' " (104). More pessimistically, Tyson reads the can's caroming as the novel's "best metaphor for the complexity of historical events, both past and current, and for the impossibility of acquiring any sure knowledge of them" (19).

H37.25, B23.18 a silvery, reticulated bloom of glass According to Tyson, the mirror represents the Lacanian "mirror stage" of development, in which the sense of self is reflected back to the individual as a stable unity. Here, that reflection is shattered, representing the individual's initiation into the symbolic order, the next stage of development. See H41.23n for more on this.

H40.16, B25.22 as we leave milk While Irish folklore is replete with tales involving the propitiation of leprechauns, I have been unable to find any specific reference to the leaving of milk for that purpose.

H41.12, B26.7 shivaree A corruption of "charivari," meaning a confused babel, deriving from the practice of serenading an unpopular marriage with "music" played on saucepans, kettles, trays, etc. (*OED*). It is not clear whether this is a commentary on Oedipa's fledgling relationship with Metzger or simply a measure of the Paranoids' incompetence.

H41.20, B26.15 Things grew less and less clear. On one level, of course, this is hardly surprising. Between the two of them, Oedipa and Metzger have polished off a bottle of Beaujolais, a bottle of tequila, and what sounds like the best part of a bottle of bourbon. The wonder is that Oedipa is still walking.

On a less literal level, though, the gradual stripping away of the layers of insulation with which she has armored herself against Metzger suggests what is to come for Oedipa in the course of her investigations into the Tristero. The revelations that she pursues are indeed couched initially in terms of a kind of striptease show (H54.14n), and when she finally articulates her sense of the failure of her sexual relationships, she says that her men are "stripping" from her (H152.32n).

H41.23, B26.17   a moment of nearly pure terror   "As usual, there is a double meaning here, besides the breaking of a mirror and the popular superstition involved. Oedipa has already lost track of her image, or 'imago,' in the Lacanian sense. She wants to get beyond the mirror or through it, like Alice, into another world" (Colville 36). "Her looking in mirrors can . . . be read as a desire to capture the stable, unified version of herself she once knew, a desire to return to the safety of the [Lacanian] Imaginary Order" (Tyson 20).

H41.25, B26.20   "I'll be 35."   Which makes Oedipa twenty-eight in 1964, Pynchon's age.

H42.2, B26.30   impaling one another on bayonets   A slightly fanciful chain of associations might link this moment with Oedipa's later encounter with John Nefastis. The mention of the phallic bayoneting that is occurring on screen coincides with Oedipa's noticing Metzger's erection and with what appears to be sexual arousal on her part. Nefastis will invite Oedipa to have intercourse with him in front of the television, though this time the stimulus will be less violent—merely the thought of the fecundity of the Chinese (H108.3). On the latter occasion, however, Oedipa flees in horror.

H42.12, B26.39   Barbie doll   "They both uncannily change sizes in Oedipa's mind, somewhat like Alice when she drinks from her bottle. He is a 'scaled-up' girl, and she is an even more 'scaled-up' doll. He is turned into a little girl, and she is turned into a sexless toy. These similes indicate Oedipa's lack of psychological or sexual involvement in what she is doing; sex is a kind of joke" (Couturier 24).

H42.12, B26.39   She may have fallen asleep   Rundle cites this as one of a number of moments throughout the novel when the narrative voice appears to lose authority, "producing an unsettling oscillation between acceptance and rejection of the novel's fictional world" (32).

H42.21, B27.7   Her climax   "This climax punningly dramatizes the way in which the media have now 'penetrated' Oedipa, impregnating her with the desire to see how they relate to each other. The scene in the motel is thus a comic but crucially important preliminary stage to Oedipa's search where the multiple layers of protective clothing are stripped away and where the self is revealed as being in unavoidable contact with its own technological environment" (Seed 118–19).

Berressem has a similar response: "In this meeting of human and machinic *jouissance*, human and electronic levels are conflated within a sexual agenda" (86).

⊸◁ Chapter 3

H44.3, B28.3 Tristero   Seed has noted the stylistic characteristics of the passage in which we first come across the name of this strange, shadowy organization. "Pynchon constantly draws back from attributing too definite an awareness to Oedipa. The Jamesian periphrastic tenses ('was to label,' 'would come to haunt,' etc.) suggest a knowledge of subsequent events—Pynchon is not tying himself rigidly to the moment—and yet the tone of the passage reflects Oedipa's early sense of puzzlement, rather like Alice in Wonderland, as the first sentence hints" (129). Petillon suggests an even stronger connection with James, arguing that the Tristero is "highly reminiscent of the London anarchist underground James described in *his* novel about the disinherited, *The Princess Cassamassima.*" Petillon also points out that "Pynchon's technique . . . follows, in broad outline, James's rule: 'My scheme called for the suggested nearness (to all our apparently ordered life) of some sinister anarchic underworld, heaving in its pain, its power and its hate: a presentation, not of sharp particulars, but of loose appearances, vague motions and sounds and symptoms, just perceptible presences and general looming possibilities' " (140). Dugdale quotes the same passage (124).

Seed's reference to the "repeatedly tentative nature of [the novel's] narrative comments ('if . . . as if,' etc.)" is certainly in line with the Jamesian "scheme." The Tristero is revealed to Oedipa in tantalizing fragments, none of them sufficient to constitute definitive evidence of even the existence of a whole, let alone its shape. This passage anticipates not only the uncertainty with which Oedipa will be faced but also one of the possibilities that will occur to her by the end of the novel. The suggestion that her discovery of the Tristero might have an object is sufficient to indicate that her quest may be determined, and the possibility that the object might be to free her from her tower would indicate that the agent of her liberation is acting counter to the magic that had held her prisoner. (This is consistent with Nohrnberg's observation that the Tristero's somewhat "charismatic" nature makes it akin to the Counterforce that will oppose the activities of the Firm in *Gravity's Rainbow* [154]).

From the very beginning, it seems, certainty about the Tristero is hard to come by. It is hardly surprising, therefore, that interpretations of its significance should vary. As with the characters, critics have sought a key to the Tristero through the etymological possibilities of its name. Mendelson, for example, suggests that "its name hides not only the unseen (and, to the secular world, illicit) relationship of the *tryst*, but also the *tristesse* that must accompany any sense of coherence and fullness" (141). Palmeri is more or less in agreement, though he sees "tryst" as implying "sinister adventure" and derives the name's "melancholy" aspect from "tristia" rather than Mendelson's "tristesse" (988). Tanner finds "triste" in the name and adds "terror" to it, thus giving a name that "represents both the sadness and terror of America" ("V." 43). Given the failure of love that the novel chronicles, the derivation "triste" and "eros" does not seem too farfetched.

Petillon suggests an elaborate network of literary allusions, stemming from Eliot's reference in *The Waste Land* to *"le Prince d'Aquitaine a la tour abolie."* "This line itself bears a cryptic reference to Gerard de Nerval's poem 'El Deschidado,' in which most of the major themes of the Tristero are sounded (the exile into a shadowy, marginal world; the former prince whose 'tower' has been 'abolished'; the 'black sun of melancholia'). Nerval's poem, in turn, takes its title from the motto on the shield of the mysterious Disinherited Knight who turns up at the beginning of Walter

Scott's *Ivanhoe*, and who will eventually represent both the Saxons and the Jews evicted from their estates by Norman chivalry" (144).

For Madsen, the Tristero represents for Oedipa everything that does not fit within "the explanatory reach of her sense of meaning." It is "a sign of an alternative world view, or, in allegoric terms, a pretextual alternative to Oedipa's orthodox interpretation of her world" (56).

Mackey associates the Tristero with the "profane mysteries" enumerated by Marc Edmund Jones: the Avatar, the Chosen People, Prophecy, and Signatures. According to Mackey, Tristero himself, the founder of the organization, represents the Avatar, the person whose life provides an "ideal pattern" for would-be initiates to follow. "The lost Americans of the novel are the chosen people here," while the post horn becomes the symbol of prophecy through its association with the trumpet of apocalypse. The Signatures are represented by the various signs of the Tristero that Oedipa encounters. These profane mysteries, Mackey argues, are a veil covering the sacred mysteries to which only the persistent few may gain access (34–35).

At the simplest level, opinions about the Tristero differ in only one regard: the organization is ultimately viewed as either positive or negative in its influence on Oedipa or on society as a whole. Among those who see it in a positive light, Mendelson is perhaps the most unequivocal, associating the Tristero with the idea of the sacred and asserting that it provides Oedipa with the means to perceive a degree of coherence in her world that has hitherto been hidden from her. The Tristero, Mendelson argues, is always associated with "the language of the sacred," and its foils are always associated with "sacrality gone wrong" (117). Along the same lines, though more narrowly, Watson insists that the novel "persistently implies" that the Tristero is "analogous to Christianity" (68). While Mendelson acknowledges that the Tristero has its demonic side, he insists that this does not "contradict the Trystero's potentially sacred significance: the demonic is a subclass of the sacred, and exists, like the sacred, on a plane of meaning different from the profane and the secular" (122).

The notion that the Tristero may occupy a different "plane of meaning" coincides with the concept of revelation as it unfolds in the novel. Revelation, we will come to see, constitutes the intrusion into one world of information that originates in a different world (see, in particular, H120.7n, Oedipa's encounter with Jesús Arrabal). Whether these "worlds" can be identified in purely religious terms—that is, as sacred and secular—is a matter of interpretation, but the fundamental equation of revelation with renewal is not affected either way. Schaub makes the link between revelation and thermodynamics in seeing the Tristero as the source of vital, regenerative energy for Oedipa. He also appears to share Nohrnberg's association of the Tristero with some kind of organized resistance to the stultifying forces that control contemporary life: "There are two requirements . . . for regenerating a system: the energy must come from an Outside, and it must be different from the energy present Inside. This is the importance of Tristero; for it represents the possible infusion from the outside of an organized 'difference' reinstating opposition. The success of Oedipa's sorting rests directly on the uncertainty over the source of the information she accumulates and organizes into the Tristero; for if these clues do not originate in a system or culture outside the one Oedipa seeks to redeem, then they are only part of the inside system which is running down" (32). Kolodny and Peters take a similar position, arguing that the Tristero is "another dimension of consciousness and a truer means of communication" (86).

Others regard the Tristero more negatively, giving prominence to the darker side of its apparent activities. Eddins offers a corrective to Mendelson's view: "When Mendelson asserts that 'the foils to Trystero (sic) are always associated with sacrality gone wrong,' he obscures the important datum that Trystero itself has just this association. It practices assassination and mind-control in the name of its own self-righteous gnostic usurpations, and is explicitly identified by one group as the demiurgic hierarchy responsible for a fallen cosmos" (96). Henkle's view is very similar, though he seems certain that Pynchon's intentions are humorous: "Tristero is another rendition—comic, of course—of what

Fiedler sees as the American Faustian theme: an urge to set up controls and intricate systems in order to acquire overweening power" (104). Abernethy associates the Tristero with an "Augustinian" entropy, arguing that it is simply part of "the closed system of America" and thus has no capacity to regenerate the lives of those who await its coming to power (22).

While most critics finally settle for either a predominantly negative or a predominantly positive view of the Tristero, many are willing to concede that what Oedipa discovers is not uniformly good or bad. Eddins, for example, while arguing that the Tristero is ultimately "more demiurge than victim," grants that its opposition to the monopolistic practices of the state-owned mail system makes it in a very real way the "champion of Pynchon's beloved preterite" (95). Palmeri is more assertive of the doubleness associated with the Tristero, identifying three realms in which this doubleness is played out: "In political history, Tristero is revolutionary and reactionary; in economic history, it is sinister and saddening; in the religious realm, it includes both the sacred and the demonic" (991).

H45.1, B28.12   stamp collection   The stamps are "samples of all those dreams and substitute objects by which people avoid love and human relationships" (Tanner, "V." 42). Pierce's ability to lose himself in the exotic landscapes depicted either literally or by implication in the stamps is perhaps an echo of Oedipa's awareness that the Mexico to which she believes she has escaped is simply a fabrication of her own imagination. The "escape" that Pierce achieves through the stamps is equally illusory.

Slade regards the stamps as offering "one more fragment of Pierce's Calvinism, his habit of substituting cosmic vision for love" (156).

H45.10, B29.3   Yet . . . sensitized   The narrative stance is odd here; the "Yet" appears to indicate a desire to excuse Oedipa for her failure to recognize the significance of the stamps right away, even though the reader is hardly likely to suppose that she should do so. Furthermore, the effect of "set up or sensitized" and the anticipatory reference to "the other, almost offhand things" is to create the illusion that Oedipa is already beginning to think of her situation in terms that will only later characterize her attitude toward the Tristero and Pierce's legacy. We are perhaps being reminded both of Oedipa's feeling that her encounter with Metzger was less than spontaneous and of her sense of meanings being generated just beyond her capacity to grasp them.

H45.21, B29.13   nothing much to say   Watson notes that we can assume from the letter's postmark that it has been sent via Tristero courier (63). Like most of the mail associated with the Tristero, this one is more or less devoid of significant content—the medium, one might venture, is more important than the message.

H46.24, B30.7   POTSMASTER   Seed argues that the misprint is a "crucial" detail, "since it suggests that Pynchon is drawing attention to communication as an act or process rather than as a quantity (information or content) which is transferred from place to place" (141). Berressem attaches a similar importance to the misprint, arguing that it indicates a shift of Oedipa's attention from signified to signifier in a manner consistent with the novel's overarching acknowledgment of the world's textuality (95).

Given Pynchon's propensity for elaborate punch-line setups, however, it is clear that the *choice* of misprint was made in part to allow Metzger to get off his joke about kettles and gunboats.

H47.10, B30.23   the stillness of the pool   Images of stillness and blankness are all part of the novel's elaborate matrix of references to high-entropy closed systems. The self-absorption of the narcissism implicit in the name of the motel is a second-order component of the same matrix.

H47.26, B30.37   Lissajous figures   Named after Jules Lissajous (1822–80), these are the curving patterns formed by two-dimensional oscillations. They are most readily observed on the screen of an oscilloscope when electrical signals are applied across its horizontal and vertical inputs.

H47.31, B31.2   this je ne sais quoi   The "sensitized" Oedipa may be overreacting, or she may be reacting to a genuine current of hostility emanating from people who appear to be part of an antimonopoly cabal.

H48.9, B31.11 "Stockhausen" Karlheinz Stockhausen, a German composer, born in 1928. In 1953 he established the Koln studio for electronic music. Cowart notes that Stockhausen and others like him were attempting to find a music that went beyond the "well-tempered scale" that was the norm, and suggests that "the work of these composers complements Pynchon's theme, for in a sense his heroine also attempts a 'breakthrough to some new scale of pitches'" (*Art of Allusion* 82).

H48.10, B31.12 Radio Cologne Stockhausen became affiliated with Radio Cologne in 1953, establishing an electronic music laboratory where he began his first experiments.

H48.19, B31.21 audio oscillators ... contact mikes A variety of electronic devices of the kind Stockhausen employed in his music. An audio oscillator is a device such as an audio frequency generator that produces electric oscillations. A gunshot machine is a machine with a highly directional pickup pattern used to gather sound from a distance, while a contact mike is a microphone designed to pick up vibrations from contact with an object or a person.

H48.21, B31.23 ax Any musical instrument, but usually a saxophone.

H48.28, B31.29 Mike Fallopian Watson regards this name, along with that of Stanley Koteks, as contributing to the book's theme of transsexuality through their references to "the anatomy and sanitation of strictly female processes" (60).

H48.29, B31.31 Peter Pinguid This comically conceived group lends itself to a number of different readings. For Abernethy, the organization is yet another manifestation of American society's tendency toward inertia: "The Peter Pinguid view of history is closed; their 'facts' echo themselves into nothingness" (31). For Nohrnberg, on the other hand, the Peter Pinguid Society is a type or instance of the Tristero, one of the many such secret or semisecret groups Oedipa will encounter in the course of her quest.

The name contains another typical Pynchon pun. "Pinguid" means "abounding in fat; unctuous, greasy, oily" (*OED*). Commodore Pinguid, therefore, can be seen as something of a "greasy prick."

H49.I, B31.36 "They?" . . . "Us?" Leland sees this exchange as typical of the novel's preoccupation with the futility of all our attempts to "find in language a non-linguistic map of reality" (52). Exchanges such as this, he argues, "involve the linguistic interaction between subject and object where both are dynamic and subject to the arbitrary nature of the medium employed. At the level of language, the words 'they' and 'us' do not signify existential persons but instead are 'unfulfilled' and empty grammatical categories. Oedipa's question reaches to the heart of the emptiness, yet her attempts to 'fill' the void and purge the order of words of its essential ambiguity fail" (52).

H49.13, B32.7 Nicholas II of Russia An uncharacteristic lapse on Pynchon's part. He presumably meant Alexander II, since Nicholas did not become Czar until 1894.

H49.I5, B3I.9 Rear Admiral Popov A typical mixing of fact with fiction. Russian naval vessels were berthed in San Francisco in the fall of 1863—one of the corvettes, the *Novich*, was wrecked on Point Keys in September of that year—and Nicholson notes that the commander of the Russian fleet in the Pacific from 1854 (in fact, 1858) was one Alexandrovitch Popov (99). Peter Pinguid and the *Disgruntled*, on the other hand, appear to be Pynchon's inventions.

H49.20, B32.I4 "Alabama" . . . "Sumter" Wild rumors indeed. Neither vessel ever got closer to California than the coast of Brazil. Nonetheless, home guard units were formed to fend off possible attacks on the harbor by Confederate raiders.

H49.29, B32.23 not too clear "The Pinguid records are a comic parody of the unreliability (the relativity) of historical records, mimicked by the either/or prose of the narrator" (Schaub 33).

Dugdale speculates that Pynchon may be parodying "the events of 2–3 August 1964, the so-called first and second Tonkin Gulf incidents (the latter entirely fictive), which Johnson used as a pretext to launch bombing strikes and acquire new powers to conduct the war in secret" (155). Other targets identified by Dugdale include the John Birch society's "myth of martyrdom" and "Aristotle's sea battle, which is at the centre of discussion of either/or logic and excluded middles" (199n).

H49.30, B32.24 "Bogatir" . . . "Gaidamak" The *bogatyri* are the heroes of the old Russian oral epics, young, strong, and aggressive in defense of Russia. The *gaidamaki*, or *haidamaki*, were originally the cossack and peasant forces that defended the eighteenth-century Ukraine against Polish aggression. Later, this was the name adopted by the anti-Bolshevik forces of the Ukraine in 1918–19.

H50.8, B32.34 Krasnyi Arkhiv Red Archive. This is in fact the title of a Soviet journal that was published from 1922 to 1941. Pynchon appears to assume that it is the name of a central records depository.

H50.20, B33.6 the Birch Society Founded in December 1958 by Robert Welch, the anticommunist organization gets its name from Captain John Birch, a Baptist missionary in China who was recruited for intelligence work during World War II. He was killed by an officer of the Communist Chinese army while engaged in an obscure mission near Hsuchow on August 25, 1945. Fallopian's "fanatic" probably derives from Birch's rigid fundamentalist beliefs.

H51.21, B33.38 "During the drought that year" By "the heart of dowtown L.A." Fallopian presumably means the heart of what is the present city. The drought of 1864, the third year of drought following the floods of 1860–61, proved disastrous for a large number of landholders in the county. Huge tracts of land were sold to speculators in lieu of seemingly trifling tax debts.

H52.13, B34.21 WASTE Critics have been more than willing to demonstrate the truth of Pütz's claim that this is "a multi-function signifier" (378). In keeping with the ambiguity that surrounds the Tristero, Pearce wonders whether this apparent manifestation of the organization's presence in contemporary America "is a comic triumph of the underground or if W.A.S.T.E. is not finally the product of the giant aero-space corporation itself" (222). He suggests that Inverarity's holding of stock in Yoyodyne would tend to push us in the direction of the latter possibility. A similar view is held by Coates: "If WASTE may be a counter-force of the dispossessed, it may also be the posthumous executor of Pierce Inverarity's American millionaire dream of an after-life in the form of Oedipa's obsession" (127).

Eddins, too, notes a duality that he claims is implicit in the acronym: "In this sense Tristero is enthalpic, taking the silent human 'waste' left by social entropy and using it with the energy of vital exchange. Thus, the old sailor can write to his wife, the mother to her son, with a candor and power that must otherwise be suppressed.

"The other side of the gnostic opposition, however, is invoked by the 'Empire' aspect of Tristero, implying as it does that the ominously 'Silent' oppressed 'Await' their turn to institute their own system of absolute control" (95).

Coates links the acronym with the shift in cultural practices associated with the move to the New World: "Once a culture founded on mobility came into being . . . it became possible to dream of leaving one's waste behind; and this is what happens in the United States, a culture that throws away things rather than repairing them, replicating thereby the initial gesture of departure from the native land" (126).

Decker notes the relevance of Pynchon's essay on Watts, published shortly after *Lot 49*, to the waste motif that develops in the novel: "Pynchon is interested . . . in the creative and communicative potential of the waste and debris accumulated by Watts residents in the wake of the riots" (35).

An organization by the same name appears in John Kendrick Bangs's *Alice in Blunderland* (1907). There, the intials stand for "Wisdom, Acclaim and Status Through Expenditures."

H52.15, B34.23 a symbol she'd never seen before Both Tanner ("Crying" 186) and Mendelson (132) build on religious connotations associated with the Tristero in agreeing that the muted horn signifies a desire to "block" or "mute" the trumpet of apocalypse. This aspect goes hand in hand with the more obvious association with muffled or altered forms of communication. "As the logotype of WASTE, a major facet of the Tristero, the muted post horn signifies silence rather than speech or writing" (Richwell, "Pynchon's *Crying*" 50). "The muted post horn, emblem of dispossession, renounces authorized channels of communication. Tristero communicates only through alteration of licensed signals: through parody or strategic silences" (Palmeri 994).

Davidson broadens the terms of the discussion to include human relationships: "The muted post horn—both verbally and pictorially an ambiguous sexual symbol—suggests that, in much of America, both communication and love are fundamentally flawed" (46).

H52.21, B34.28 hieroglyphics "A double iteration, through the prefix *hiero*, of the Trystero's sacrality" (Mendelson 127).

"The hieroglyphs indicate another world view, one that seeks connections rather than the dualistic distinctions that dominate the western intellectual tradition. In learning to translate the hieroglyphs, Oedipa rediscovers metaphor as a means of making sense. Metaphor-making is an act of imaginative creation, one that asserts similarity or connection based on the recognition of some pattern" (Newman 82).

H53.23, B35.23 his letter As with so many other aspects of the novel, the letter Fallopian receives lends itself to contradictory interpretations. One could argue, as Couturier does, that the banality of the letter draws attention more to the medium than to the message, focusing on the issue of monopolistic control over the means of communication and on the Tristero's centuries-long struggle against it (11). This view of course depends on our willingness to regard the PPS mail system as part of the Tristero/WASTE setup. Mendelson is among those who do not adopt this position, arguing rather that there are "*two* secret communications systems: the Trystero and its entirely secular counterpart, the system used by the right-wing Peter Pinguid Society" (129). Mendelson sees Fallopian's letter as evidence of the society's failure to provide anything of substance for its members to communicate about; there is no "sense of the numinous," unlike what is at least hinted at in communications associated with the Trystero (130). Fallopian's bitterness at the emptiness of his letter would seem to lend credence to Mendelson's view.

H54.I, B35.33   begun around 1845   In fact, attempts to establish a postal monopoly go back at least to 1792, when the first legislation against private mail carriers was enacted. An act of 1827 is also of relevance here since it is presumably the 1861 emendation of that act on which Fallopian bases his tentative thesis. Part of the 1827 statute provides as follows: "And be it further enacted that no person, other than the Postmaster General, or his authorized agents, shall set up any foot or horse post, for the conveyance of letters and packets, upon any post-road, which is or may be established as such by law; and every person who shall offend herein, shall incur a penalty not exceeding fifty dollars, for each letter or packet so carried" (4 Stat. 238, section 3 [March 2, 1827]).

This injunction was elaborated on in the legislation of 1845, which represented a major effort on the part of the Post Office Department to dam up the flow of revenues to the private carriers: "And be it further enacted, That it shall not be lawful for any person or persons to establish any private express or expresses for the conveyance, nor in any manner to cause to be conveyed, or provide for the conveyance or transportation by regular trips, or at stated periods or intervals, from one city, town, or other place, to any other city, town, or other place in the United States, between from and to which cities, towns, or other places the United States mail is regularly transported under the authority of the Post Office Department, of any letters, packets, or packages of letters, or other matter properly transportable in the United States mail" (5 Stat. 735, section 9 [March 3, 1845]). The fine for violators of this provision was $150 for each letter carried. The act also explicitly prohibited the use of "stage-coach, railroad car, steamboat, packet boat, or other vehicle or vessel" that traveled regular post routes for the transportation of mail other than the official mail.

While it is a little puzzling that Fallopian regards 1861 as the year in which the government set out on a campaign of "vigorous suppression," it is possible that he is referring to a provision in the act of March 2 that plugged a large loophole in the 1827 and

1845 regulations by extending those regulations to cover "all post routes which have been, or may hereafter be, established in any town or city by the Postmaster General" (12 Stat. 204, section 4 [March 2, 1861]). Before this act, regulations had covered only post routes *between* towns and cities.

Since a number of different pieces of legislation governing the operation of the mail routes were passed in the years that Pynchon singles out here, it is difficult to know exactly which ones he is referring to. It is probable, however, that he has in mind the legislation that at various times established specific post routes throughout the country, thus bringing a network of routes legally within the control of the Post Office. It is interesting that he does not note the act of 1855, which designated, one by one, some six thousand official post routes in states and territories from coast to coast.

H54.14, B36.6   some unique performance   "It is an amazing passage, shifting in tone from vaudeville frivolity to a melodramatic note which is in fact quite chilling. But one important point to note is the conflation of 'performance' with 'historical figuration.' History and theatre become almost interchangeable terms, and Oedipa will never know when she is, or is not, present at some kind of 'performance'—a 'play' which might end in harmless concluding knockabout, or with her hearing 'words she never wanted to hear.' Just what kind of 'performance' is America putting on anyway? All fun and jollity—or something 'malign and pitiless' coming down the aisles? When—if—history is 'undressed,' what will it look like?" (Tanner, "Crying" 179).

Both Schaub and Watson see the explicit link with the strip Botticelli game (H36.6n) as evidence of a connection between Oedipa and the Tristero. For Schaub, this takes the form of an "inescapable suspicion that Oedipa and Tristero are somehow involved in one another, and that Oedipa herself—as the name suggests—may be at the heart of the declining society" (36). Watson attributes a similar suspicion to Oedipa herself: "The Tristero-as-stripper metaphor, given the precedent of the Strip Botticelli game, suggests Oedipa's subliminal fear that she will be exposed as a manifestation of Tristero" (62).

Mendelson reads the passage as emblematic of "two different concepts of art." The possible endings posited for the Tristero's "performance" are equivalent to art's capacity to delight and/or instruct and thus, in Mendelson's view, to the distinction between what he calls "subjunctive" fiction and "indicative" fiction (139).

H55.17, B36.39   the unimaginable Pacific   These musings, which come to be associated implicitly with Oedipa, are reminiscent of some of Dennis Flange's in Pynchon's early story "Low-lands": "If the sea's tides are the same that not only wash along your veins but also billow through your fantasies then it is all right to listen but not to tell stories about that sea" (273).

H55.29, B37.11   some unvoiced idea   Eddins draws attention to the tentative nature of Oedipa's "dream of Pacific redemption" (100), noting that it is described as an "arid hope." Tyson reads the dream as "nostalgia for Nature as the source and sign of the [Lacanian] Imaginary Order, of a stable, unified self in a stable, unified world" (20).

H56.5, B37.18   the usual hieratic geometry   Presumably the word "usual" is to be ascribed to Oedipa, who has apparently very quickly become accustomed to perceiving the possibility of significance in the configurations of her surroundings.

H56.9, B37.22   ogived and verdigrised   An "ogive" is a pointed arch. "Verdigrised" indicates that the building is either roofed with copper that has oxidized to the familiar blue-green color or has been painted to seem as though this is the case.

H58.3, B39.2   Anthony Giunghierrace   Since the Italian for "jaguar" is "giaguaro," there does not appear to be a clear connection between this name and "Tony Jaguar."

H58.6, B39.5   "Eh, sfacim'"   Derived from "sfacimento," meaning dissolution or decay, the expression is probably best translated as "Ah, shit."

H58.8, B39.7   "Adeste Fideles"   Latin title of "O Come All Ye Faithful."

H58.23, B39.21   Darrowlike   Clarence Seward Darrow (1857–1938), a Chicago lawyer noted for his flamboyant appeals to juries. Darrow is remembered for his role in the so-called "monkey trial" of

J. T. Scopes, the Tennessee teacher accused of violating the law by teaching evolution.

H59.17, B40.9   crushed, plastic foam   Styrofoam had been manufactured by Dow since the early fifties. Either Pynchon was unfamiliar with the name, or cups made of styrofoam were a relatively recent phenomenon.

H61.1, B41.19   "Human bones"   The bones form what Palmeri calls the "narrative kernel" of the economic aspects of Tristero. He enumerates five occurrences of the motif: the Lost Guard of Faggio in *The Courier's Tragedy* (H68.23), the massacre of the coach passengers witnessed by Diocletian Blobb (H157.24), the Wells, Fargo party wiped out by marauders in black uniforms (H89.14), the American soldiers who died on the shores of the Lago di Pietà (H61.30), and the bones taken from the cemetery torn up to make way for the freeway. "All five instances of the narrative kernel relate sinister metamorphoses: the bones of the dead are transformed into charcoal, boneblack, ink, and eventually decorate the bottom of an ersatz lake" (991). While the general pattern that Palmeri discerns seems undeniable, I do not share his apparent certainty that Inverarity used bones from the cemetery—the exchange between Metzger and Di Presso is ambiguous on this score (H61.13). Nor is it altogether established that the bogus Indians recalled by Mr. Thoth as having stirred boneblack with their feathers (H92.11n) are at all the same as the marauders in black uniforms who attacked the Wells, Fargo party.

H61.22, B41.40   Lago di Pietà   I have been unable to locate a lake by this name. Pynchon could be referring to any one of a number of such small-scale battles that took place during the slow and costly Allied advance on Rome in 1943–44.

H61.28, B42.6   (in 1943 tragic)   "This tragedy, prefigured in Wharfinger's play, has a central function in the novel; it shows the process whereby death loses its magic and stops being the ultimate source of symbolic exchange, and is turned into a text. If the skeletons had remained in their watery tomb, they would have continued to live in the imagination of their country. Beaconsfield and Inverarity have killed the G.I.s a second time: they have robbed them

of their symbolic value, to give them a commercial value instead"
(Couturier 16).

H62.1, B42.11 plunging, enfilading fire That is, firing from above
and along a line of troops.

H62.5, B42.15 Stuka A dive bomber, used to great effect by the
German air force in World War II.

H62.27, B42.36 Forest Lawn The reference is to one or more of four
"memorial parks" by this name, all located in Southern California.
The first of them was founded in Glendale in 1914.

H62.29, B42.38 Senator McCarthy Joseph Raymond McCarthy
(1908–57) made a name for himself as an anticommunist crusader
in the early fifties. Jaguar's understatement—"having achieved a
certain ascendancy over the rich cretini"—and his "dim" association of McCarthy with an inflated and ubiquitous jingoism are
some indication of the rapidity with which McCarthyism lost
credibility.

H63.9, B43.9 menhaden An extremely prolific marine fish used in
the production of fertilizer.

H63.12, B43.12 Fort Wayne Home, it will be recalled, of the Fort
Wayne Settecento Ensemble, whose rendering of the Vivaldi Kazoo
Concerto accompanies Oedipa on her shopping trip at the begin-
ning of the novel (H10.28).

H63.26, B43.26 "They've been listening" Di Presso's exaggerated
paranoia is comic, but coming as it does in conjunction with the
coincidence of the bones in the lake, it perhaps serves to make us
sensitive to the possibility of patterns of significance beyond those
afforded by chance juxtapositions.

H64.26, B44.18 *The Courier's Tragedy* Couturier suggests that the
play serves a function similar to that of the "Mousetrap" in Ham-
let: "It reflects the main plot and contributes to quicken its pace"
(17). Tanner notes the appropriateness of the title to a play about
"competing 'communications' systems" ("Crying" 181).

H64.27, B44.18 Wharfinger I am indebted to my colleague, Dr.
Sidney Sondergard, for the ingenious suggestion that Pynchon may
have consciously or unconsciously conflated the names of a number of seventeenth-century tragedians—Webster, Heywood, Mar-
ston, Ford, and Massinger—to arrive at his fictional playwright.

Both Cowart (*Art of Allusion* 105) and Colville (30) point out that the name means the manager of a commercial wharf. Cowart wants to associate the name with Driblette's suicide—"one tends to think of it as 'wharf-finger'—i.e., a jetty or pier-style wharf pointing like a finger into the deep." Colville simply notes that we first learn of the name at the Fangoso Lagoons marina.

H65.1, B44.25 the Tank Couturier supposes that the theater's name "probably refers to the war, as does the playwright's name, Wharfinger" (17). He also takes note of the theater's location, as does Tanner (citing Kermode), between two firms having to do with "information gathering and broadcasting" (Couturier 17), "circulation and communication" (Tanner, "Crying" 181).

H65.14, B44.37 so preapocalyptic The sense of imminent apocalypse that pervades *V.*, as well as our own sense of the nature of cold war fearfulness, enable us to recognize some similarities between Wharfinger's first audiences and those who attend the play in San Narciso. Seed suggests that the play itself, or at least the genre of Jacobean melodrama, "supplies Pynchon with a means of dramatizing Cold War Paranoia in offering him conspiratorial patterns to mimic" (121).

H65.18, B45.1 Angelo, then So begins Pynchon's summary of the wonderfully convoluted plot of the play. Olsen may be a little wide of the mark when he maintains that the convolutions are what is important, rather than the play itself (79), though there can be no doubt that many readers have found the world of *The Crying of Lot 49* every bit as labyrinthine as Wharfinger's "landscape of evil." The thematic parallels between the play and Oedipa's quest are sufficiently compelling to discourage any separation of structure from content.

H65.21, B45.4 Saint Narcissus This image of Saint Narcissus has been prefigured in the novel (H23.3n), as has the associated allusion to the myth of Narcissus. Palmeri claims that Eusabius's account of the miracles associated with the bishop provides a paradigm that competes with the classical myth, setting the "potency of miracle" against "sterile self-love" (986). Oedipa will encounter Saint Narcissus again in the bedroom of the old wino (H127.15n).

H66.14, B45.29 Thurn and Taxis family It has proved extremely difficult to track down a single plausible source for Pynchon's knowledge about the Thurn and Taxis postal monopoly. One possibility is Alvin F. Harlow's *Old Post Bags*, which devotes a chapter to this "remarkable family of postmen." Berthe Delepinne's account of the Thurn and Taxis family's role in the history of Belgian postal services may also have caught Pynchon's eye as he browsed the shelves in the library at Cornell.

H66.28, B46.4 Francesca is Pasquale's mother Quite apart from its function as an accurate component of Pynchon's parody, this incest motif serves as a symbolic pointer to the closed-system characteristics of the world of the play, while at the same time it establishes links with Oedipa's own world—most explicitly through the "endless, convoluted incest" that horrifies Mucho during his time at the car lot (H14.30n). Readers may be reminded of Duke Ferdinand's desire for his sister in *The Duchess of Malfi*, the incestuous union of Giovanni and his sister Annabella in Ford's *'Tis Pity She's a Whore*, and Spurio's affair with his stepmother in *The Revenger's Tragedy*.

H68.5, B47.4 zany Paraclete One of a number of allusions to Pentecost associated with the central issues of communication and revelation. Here, of course, the gift of tongues is cruelly inverted, creating dark parody (Mendelson 134), a "parodic reflection of the Holy Ghost as gnostic demiurge" (Eddins 96).

Mendelson quotes the relevant passage from Acts 2: "When the day of Pentecost had come, [the Apostles] were . . . all filled with the Holy Spirit and began to speak in other tongues, as the Spirit gave them utterance. . . . The multitude came together and they were bewildered, because each one heard them speaking in his own language. . . . And all were amazed and perplexed, saying to one another, 'What does all this mean?' But others mocking said, 'They are filled with new wine'" (134, Mendelson's ellipses).

H69.17, B48.9 locked up in his patrician hothouse A typical image of enclosure and the dissipation of energy. See also H73.31n and H75.17n.

H70.4, B48.29 felt threatened As Tanner notes (*City of Words* 176), Oedipa is equally disturbed by the absence of meaning as she is by its presence.

H71.24, B50.2 either literally or as metaphor As most commentators have noted, Pynchon's work invites analysis in terms of paired opposites, and *Lot 49* is no exception. Here we are reminded of one such binary set, literal versus metaphorical, and "like Oedipa, are teased and drawn into a new and problematic area of semantic dubiety—between the literal and metaphorical" (Tanner, "Crying" 178). The ambiguity that creeps into the play as soon as the Tristero becomes the implicit object of attention is consistent with the indeterminacy that will frustrate Oedipa's attempts to pin the Tristero down, and it anticipates her later musings about "excluded middles" (H181.19).

H73.22, B51.23 in lithe and terrible silence This appearance of the Tristero assassins does much to validate Oedipa's subsequent sense of the darker side of the shadowy organization she is trying to identify. The men in black mohair whom she faces at the end of the novel may or may not be agents of the Tristero, but they have been foreshadowed by Driblette's actual representation on stage of the threatening forces implicit in Wharfinger's verses.

H73.31, B51.31 ritually locks all his exits As does Pasquale earlier (H69.17n). See H75.17n for more on this image of enclosure.

H74.11, B52.4 now miraculously a long confession Mendelson reads the transformation of the letter as "a version of the miracle of Pentecost" (138), a reading that Seed regards as somewhat "solemn," given the "comical violation of probability" that has taken place (122). For Palmeri, the metamorphosis is a reminder of the story of Saint Narcissus, with its "miraculous conversion of lies into truths" (986).

H75.3, B52.30 *Tacit lies the gold once-knotted horn* The curious interplay between historical reality and the imagined world of the novel is subtly in evidence in this line. The punning on Thurn and Taxis, typical of the dramatic language that Pynchon so accurately parodies, serves to link the actual postal service of the time with the imaginary Tristero, whose muted post horn symbol is one of the earliest clues that Oedipa encounters.

H75.5, B52.32 *his tryst with Trystero* Mendelson, going along with the spirit of the novel, suggests that "the naming of the Trystero on one particular night may have been directed *at* Oedipa—that the production was not simply made available to whomever happened to buy a ticket" (137).

H75.17, B53.4   the colorless administrator   The play has depicted a world in which massive energies are gradually being dissipated in more and more uncontrolled bursts, until all that is left is a mass of bodies, presided over by the gray-clad Gennaro—a reminder, surely, of the "gray dressing of ash" that characterizes the world of Mucho's car lot (H14.14n). We have already seen Pasquale and Angelo lock themselves away to hold last, desperate orgies (H69.17, H73.31). These symbolic closed systems are familiar images in Pynchon's work, from the parties in "Mortality and Mercy in Vienna" and "Entropy" through Foppl's siege party in *V.*, and they are part of the continuum of Pynchon's preoccupation with the tendency of our culture to exhaust its potential beyond the capacity for renewal.

H75.33, B53.18   "God protect me"   Davidson reads this as typical of the many instances in which pressure is brought to bear on Oedipa to stay in her "proper" place" (41). Readers may be startled at first by Metzger's reaction, which seems old-fashioned at best and utterly irrational at worst. It is hard to see why Oedipa's desire to pursue an odd coincidence should be indicative of a radical sensibility. It turns out that Metzger is fearful that she may turn up something detrimental to Pierce Inverarity and therefore in conflict with her role as executrix of his estate.

H76.6, B53.23   "a Young Republican"   A reminder of the middle-class orientation with which Oedipa is approaching these early stages of her quest; entirely consistent with Tupperware parties, fondue, and whiskey sours.

H76.7, B53.25   "Hap Harrigan comics"   Oedipa would hardly have had much time to absorb the kind of gung-ho attitude Metzger ascribes to her, at least from the comic-strip adventures of Hop (not Hap) Harrigan, which, according to Weisenburger, were briefly chronicled in a syndicated strip only in 1941 (74). She could, however, have kept up with Hop's adventures on the radio for the next eight years.

H77.12, B54.21 gray Gennaro outfit See H75.17n for the significance of Driblette's costume.

H77.18, B54.27 incredible network of lines Once again Oedipa confronts a potential source of enlightenment in the form of a grid or network that "seems" to be capable of communicating knowledge. Like the streets of San Narciso (H24.25n) and the map of Fangoso Lagoons (H31.28n), Driblette's eyes urge Oedipa toward revelation.

H78.17, B55.18 Something came to her viscera Driblette's remark about the second copy of the book seems harmless enough on the face of it, so Oedipa's momentary alarm and her suspicion that he may be putting her on are presumably a response to his amused expression and the deliberateness with which he speaks. Clearly, she is becoming rapidly more sensitive to such apparent "clues"—or she is becoming increasingly paranoid. Her hastily blurted "Who else?" is another instance of her growing sense that she is involved in a matrix of interrelated circumstances whose meaning she feels she must elucidate.

H78.21, B55.21 "interested in texts" "The question can imply either that Oedipa is just part of the scholarly dispute surrounding the text, or that Driblette has been asked by someone, for unknown reasons, to pronounce these particular lines for this performance" (Johnston 63).

Our own (scholarly or otherwise) interest in Pynchon's text is, in any case, called into question at this moment.

H78.26, B55.27 a familiar smile Since the smile is clearly contrived—it belongs to the world of the play, a world created out of Driblette's head to some extent—we can perhaps sympathize with Oedipa's response ("cold corpse-fingers of grue"), which itself seems to belong to the world of the play. As Seed points out, it is "as if she has become infected with the play's own vocabulary" (121).

H79.10, B56.2 So hung up with words Driblette appears to be arguing here against exegesis, and since we are always as readers implicitly involved in a quest parallel to Oedipa's, we might be inclined to feel that Pynchon is speaking to us through him. Driblette's earlier claim that the play "isn't literature" and that "it doesn't mean anything" (77) adds weight to his anti-interpretive outburst, and it may be that we are already inclined to see Oedipa as a potential Stencil, that "architect-by-necessity of intrigues and breathings-together."

Critics, however, tend to reject any such identification of Driblette with his creator. Seed, for example, suggests that Driblette is simply "warning . . . Oedipa of the addictive nature of her search" (123), while Schaub argues that we should be skeptical of Driblette's discouraging posture, which is rendered suspect by his apparent reluctance to speak about the Tristero (34).

H79.19, B56.10 "I'm the projector" The parallel with the Remedios Varo painting is inescapable and has given further cause for readers to doubt Driblette as a source of valid knowledge. "Whatever the momentary attraction of this creative energy, it finally amounts to an imprisoning solipsism like that of the women in the Remedios Varos [sic] murals that had saddened Oedipa in Mexico, the world as a tapestry embroidered by captive maidens who can know only their own embroidery" (Eddins 99). "This explanation would seem to make Driblette himself a projector of worlds, as Oedipa herself may be an embroiderer of tapestries, and she cannot bear to have her vision of total alienation confirmed" (Hite 84). "Varo's painting and Driblette threaten Oedipa with the possibility that there is no meaning beyond the one she herself weaves" (Schaub 34). Schaub adds, though, that there is no confirmation or denial of this possibility, a fact which contributes to the ambiguity that he maintains is a characteristic feature of the novel as a whole.

Driblette's vehement assertion and the sad plight of the captive maidens have in common their contribution to the novel's concern with enclosure, with closed systems whose energy consumption is not matched by any compensatory replenishment from without.

We will be reminded of Driblette's claim very shortly when Oedipa asks herself whether she, too, should become a projector in a planetarium (H82.11n).

H79.31, B56.21 "washed down the drain into the Pacific" Given Driblette's ultimate fate, the irony of this pronouncement is perhaps a little heavy-handed.

H80.6, B56.28 The Adversary. Driblette's name for the Tristero captures its dual nature, suggesting the organization's darker, Manichaean side as well as its role as the champion of the disinherited.

H80.15, B56.37 You could waste your life Given the fact that Oedipa is about to devote herself more or less full time to the gathering of clues and the development of a thesis, this seems fairly bleak. Driblette does turn out to be right in one respect—Oedipa never learns "the truth" in the sense that she does not arrive at a single, coherent explanation of the meaning of the Tristero. However, we will probably not be persuaded at novel's end that she has wasted her life in the effort to do so. Driblette's claim seems to be part of his solipsistic epistemology rather than an accurate assessment of Oedipa's undertaking.

H80.21, B57.3 the centres of their webs The shift from the potentially meaningful network of lines that Oedipa first perceives to this indication of the entrapment that awaits her in Driblette's vision of things helps us further disengage from Driblette's pessimism.

H80.28, B57.9 wondered how accidental The temptation to be more knowing than Oedipa, to judge Driblette's apparent evasiveness as quite obviously deliberate, is strong but not easy to account for unequivocally. Despite some of the indications, already noted, that we are encouraged to view Driblette with some degree of suspicion, his exchange with Oedipa nevertheless serves as a fine example of the novel's ability to involve the reader in the uncertainties that beset its central character.

H80.31, B57.13 the whimsies of nighttime reception Note that Oedipa has not progressed so far in her "sensitization" that she would regard this coincidence as anything but a matter of whimsical chance. Later in the novel, we might suppose, she would be less likely to be so blasé.

○◁〚 Chapter 4

H81.8, B58.7 woven into The Tristero Again, the reference to the Varo painting is clear and serves to suggest that everything that Oedipa will "learn" may in fact fail to free her from the tower of her own imagination, just as Pierce had failed to liberate her from her buffered life in Kinneret.

H81.10, B58.10 an organized something This is a rather casual introduction of a speculation that will come to haunt Oedipa much later in the novel. The notion that Pierce may have used his will to cheat the effects of death on the human organism is consistent with the novel's working out of the theme of organization versus disorganization. Death puts an end to the complex differentiations that sustain biological processes and hold entropy at bay. By leaving "an organized something behind," Pierce would be making a small gesture of defiance in the face of this inevitable fact. (See also H178–79.)

H82.11, B59.4 *Shall I project a world?* Oedipa is clearly influenced by Driblette in her choice of analogy. She recalls his insistence that he is the projector in the planetarium, and wonders if she might not assume the same role in her dealings with Inverarity's estate. Notice that Oedipa is unsure whether she is likely to be *creating* an order or simply discovering a preexisting one—tracing it out on the "dome" like the reassuringly anthropomorphic shapes of the constellations.

H83.13, B59.39 Clayton ("Bloody") Chiclitz Chiclitz's nickname will seem mysterious to those readers not familiar with the threatening question, "Do you want a mouthful of bloody Chiclets?" Chiclitz first makes his appearance in *V.* as the president of the toy company that grows into Yoyodyne.

H83.29, B60.15 Contracts flee thee yet. Pynchon has apparently forgotten that, in *V.*, Yoyodyne had "more government contracts than it really knew what to do with" (226). It seems unlikely that the song is harking back to earlier, less successful days, since the first Minuteman test flight took place in 1961 and research and development on the missile did not really begin until 1958, only six years before Oedipa's visit.

H84.13, B60.32 panic growing An odd response, if one were to suppose that it is simply the result of being separated from the rest of the stockholders. Oedipa could very easily ask for directions. Her panic is presumably rooted in the unnerving sameness of everything in the office, in the uncommunicative stares of the engineers engaged in their undeviating routine. Oedipa is growing more and more sensitive to instances of stagnation in her environment.

H84.17, B60.36 Stanley Koteks Watson regards this name, along with that of Mike Fallopian (H48.28n), as contributing to the book's theme of transsexuality through their references to "the anatomy and sanitation of strictly female processes" (60).

H85.14, B61.22 "stifles your really creative engineer" The patent clause is part of the stultifying nature of the conglomerate Koteks works for, one of those companies that "subsume originality and initiative under a suffocating cloak of self-perpetuation" (Newman 70). Individuality means difference, and difference constitutes a culture's best defense against stagnation, encouraging as it does the free flow of ideas or intellectual energy. Note that Koteks implicitly identifies Nefastis as one of the few remaining "creative engineers."

H85.30, B61.36 John Nefastis Nicholson has pointed out that "Nefas means unspeakable and unpleasing to the gods" (95), suggesting that the inventor is scarcely on the side of the sacred, as Mendelson seems to suggest when he asserts that "Nefastis's unbalanced science is endorsed, shakily, by the language of belief" (126). Palmeri suggests that the name connotes someone "unholy, unclean, abominable" (982), while Abernethy sees a link with "nefarious," thus making Nefastis "someone evil or impious" (25). In Greek, "nifas" means "flake" or "snowflake." See the notes to H105–8 for a less negative view of Nefastis.

H86.3, B62.3 James Clerk Maxwell With the introduction of Maxwell and his demon we begin our attempts to grasp the novel's central and most elusive metaphor.

Maxwell, as Anne Mangel reminds us, was a nineteenth-century physicist who, in 1871, published the following speculation in his *Theory of Heat:* "Now let us suppose that . . . a vessel is divided into two portions, A and B, by a division in which there is a small hole, and that a being, who can see the individual molecules, opens and closes this hole, so as to allow only the swifter molecules to pass from A to B, and only the slower ones to pass from B to A. He will thus, without expenditure of work, raise the temperature of B and lower that of A, in contradiction to the second law of thermodynamics" (quoted in Mangel 195).

Koteks's account is a fair rendition of Maxwell's hypothesis and goes a little further than the original in clarifying the most important aspect of the thought experiment, its emphasis on the change from the random distribution of molecules in the system to their *ordered* arrangement in different regions of the system. What the demon prevents is the gradual reduction of all the molecules to a single energy level, a state that would resemble the "unvarying gray sickness" of Mucho's car-lot world and the "colorless gray" world presided over by Gennaro at the end of *The Courier's Tragedy.* In such a state, no energy would be available to perform useful work.

The difficulty for the reader lies in the fact that the demon scenario asks for a counterintuitive identification of disorder with uniformity. As Abernethy points out, in the context of thermodynamics, "disorder and chaos . . . do not mean a random jumble of things but rather uniformity, a lack of distinctions, a sameness, a lack of individuality, a tendency toward complete conformity. It is a 'steady-state' in which 'matter and energy' are evenly distributed" (20). Organization depends on the perception of difference— the demon must be able to tell the difference between fast-moving and slow-moving molecules, for example; postal workers must be able to tell the difference between one zip code and another. In a system in which no such perception is possible, no organization can be achieved. "Sorting," therefore, becomes an absolutely central metaphor, and the fact that Oedipa singles this concept out for objection is an indication of her intuitive grasp of her own predicament.

Schaub notes that Oedipa's response to Koteks establishes a connection between the novel's concern with images drawn from thermodynamics and the postal motif associated with the Tristero (28). He also quotes Norbert Wiener on the difference between nineteenth-century and contemporary physics in support of her objection:

> In nineteenth-century physics, it seemed to cost nothing to get information. The result is that there is nothing in Maxwell's physics to prevent one of his demons from furnishing its own power source. Modern physics, however, recognizes that the demon can only gain the information with which it [sorts the molecules] from something like a sense organ which for these purposes is an eye. The light that strikes the demon's eyes is not an energy-less component of mechanical motion, but shares in the main properties of mechanical motion itself. . . . In such a system, however, it will turn out that the constant collision between light and gas particles tends to bring the light and gas particles to an equilibrium. (56)

We will be obliged to return to the demon in greater detail when Oedipa finally encounters Nefastis himself (H105n).

H86.30, B62.28   The familiar Society for the Propagation of Christian Knowledge photo   Nohrnberg suggests that this picture is "virtually a silent rebuke of Nefastis's endeavor to procure a mechanical operation of the spirit" (156).

H87.23, B63.14   "In Berkeley."   "In [Oedipa's] postal system, a box number is meaningless unless it is completed by the name of the post office or the city. We assume that in the WASTE system a box number is enough; they have drawn up a map where Federal post offices and city names have been supplanted by numbers, inventing a Shadow country as it were" (Couturier 11).

H87.24, B63.15   his voice gone funny   If it were in fact to turn out that Oedipa's most paranoid fantasy were correct, and Pierce Inverarity had indeed set her up to be the patsy in some massively elaborate charade, then we would have to give Koteks a standing ovation for the subtlety of his performance. His acting, if that is what it is, is superb. Surely moments like these tend to tip the scales rather sharply in the direction of an objective reality for the

Tristero, or at least for a network of the disinherited who strongly believe in it.

H87.33, B63.23 "It's W.A.S.T.E." "So this single clue—or what [Oedipa] had thought of as a single sign—proliferates, separating itself into five equally enigmatic intials, signs: a paradigm of her quest" (Madsen 58).

H88.26, B64.9 a design ritual Kolodny and Peters argue that Pynchon's novel is a response to the kind of fate visited on creative minds by vast conglomerates like Yoyodyne (82). The inventiveness that Pynchon displays, the departure of his novel from the model laid down in the "procedures handbook" of convention, constitute a critique of our culture's capacity for suppressing what it seems to celebrate, namely individual ingenuity—what Fallopian refers to here as "the Myth of the American Inventor."

H89.3, B64.19 sounds like the surplus value theory The Marxist economic doctrine that describes capitalism in terms of its appropriation of that portion of the worker's contribution to the value of the manufactured product which exceeds the subsistence-level compensation paid the worker for his or her labor.

H89.12, B64.28 historical marker The event commemorated by the marker, recapitulating as it does the death of Niccolò on the shores of Lago di Pietà in *The Courier's Tragedy*, is also linked to the dead GIs whose bones decorate the bottom of the nearby Fangoso Lagoons lake and is thus part of that narrative kernel defined by Palmeri as the economic aspect of the Tristero (990). (See also H61.1n.)

H89.14, B64.30 *Wells, Fargo* Organized as an express company in California in 1852, just after the gold rush.

H89.26, B65.2 The phone buzzed on and on Like the blankness of the toilet walls in the theater, the silence at the other end of the phone line is potentially ominous. Even though Oedipa is not explicitly said to be alarmed, we have surely grown sensitive enough by this point not to dismiss her failure to make contact with Driblette without a second thought.

H90.1, B65.11 the first of many demurs The most obvious explanation for Oedipa's occasional and increasing reluctance to pursue clarification lies in the hints Driblette builds into his production of *The Courier's Tragedy*. There, the characters display a "ritual reluctance" to name the Tristero, clearly intimidated by the possibility of the very violence that is visited on Niccolò. In her "real" world, Oedipa has only the evidence of the attack on the Wells, Fargo contingent to suggest a similar danger, but she is nonetheless becoming attuned to nuances of significance that steer her away from certain kinds of inquiry.

We might, however, simply read her unwillingness as the product of a desire to avoid complication. If Zapf were to tell her the names of several other purchasers of the text, then Oedipa would no doubt feel obliged to track them down.

H90.8, B65.17   light further the dark face of the word   The portentousness of the language is a reflection of Oedipa's ill-defined but significant uneasiness over the apparent "pattern" that she sees emerging from the series of coincidences that has set her off on her quest. The religious resonances generated here are consistent with the already established motif of revelation, though there is a kind of tension in the way the "word" here (Tristero) is dark, while the "Word" that Oedipa is seeking is the word of revelation, and thus light-giving.

For what it is worth, the associations I see here are with Genesis 1:2—"and darkness was upon the face of the deep"; John 1:1—"In the beginning was the Word, and the Word was with God, and the Word was God"; John 1:5—"And the light shineth in darkness."

H90.29, B65.36   She would give them order, she would create constellations   An interesting duality is emerging to color our sense of Oedipa's role in the novel. The reference to constellations takes us back to Driblette (H79.19n) and to Oedipa's entry in her notebook (H82.11n). As we have noted, this takes us even further back, to the Varo painting, with all its connotations of self-enclosure and solipsism, and certainly the notion that Oedipa is obsessed with "bringing something of herself" to her task is consistent with those connotations. Koteks's brief lesson on Maxwell's Demon, however, has given us another metaphor to apply to Oedipa, one that seems to allow her to serve a more valuable function than that of the rather wistful discerner of compensatory patterns in the arbitrary distribution of the stars. As demon/sorter, perhaps, Oedipa will attempt to preserve the energy potential of Pierce's legacy, ensuring that its component parts are not subsumed into some massive, uniform structure that is as destructive of individual uniqueness as the engineering department of Yoyodyne. Of course, for many readers, skepticism about the capacity for redemption of capitalistic enterprises such as Pierce's runs high, and it may be that we can hardly feel optimistic about Oedipa's chances at this point in the novel. However, at least the demon's aim is to create an order that translates into the production of useful energy, and we may be happier with this image of Oedipa than with the earlier one.

H90.30, B65.38   Vesperhaven   From "vespers," the sixth and next to last of the canonical hours, and hence implying evening, and "haven" or safe harbor. A surprisingly straightforward name.

H91.2, B66.3   Leon Schlesinger   A film producer (1884–1949) who began in 1930 to produce animated films for Warner Brothers under the general title of *Looney Tunes*. He brought Porky Pig, Bugs Bunny, and Daffy Duck, among others, to the screen.

H91.7, B66.8   Mr Thoth   "Mr Thoth, named for the Egyptian god of scribes, resides in a nursing home and, like the state of the written word, decays" (Newman 76). The name connects with earlier references to hieroglyphics and with Oedipa's momentary association of Fangoso Lagoons with the *Book of the Dead* (H31.29n).

Madsen makes much of this name, noting that Thoth is credited with the introduction of plurality into the spoken language. He is, she maintains, a "counterpart to the Christian concept of Babel" (64). Thoth is also associated with Hermes, the god of cryptography and thus, Madsen argues, "is aligned with the Tristero, an organization which intentionally eludes articulation and any specificity of description" (66).

H91.17, B66.18   the Pony Express   Formed in April 1860 and lasting some sixteen months until the telegraph lines put it out of business, the Pony Express carried messages between St. Joseph, Missouri, and Sacramento, California, by means of relays of riders who covered as much as 250 miles a day.

H91.17, B66.18 back in the gold rush days Back, that is, in the days of the forty-niners, the participants in the most celebrated gold rush of all.

H91.27, B66.28 "all mixed in with a Porky Pig cartoon" According to Abernethy, "we can see in Mr. Thoth's reaction the myths of America echoing themselves into nothingness. The medium *is* the message here—a passivity leading to stasis. Like generations of Americans raised on cowboy films, he can no longer separate the 'real' Indians killed by his grandfather (also fakes, agents of Tristero) from the cartoon Indians" (32).

Winston identifies the cartoon as "The Blow Out," released by Warner Brothers in 1936 (74), and Mark Irwin finds it an apt emblem for the whole critical enterprise that has grown up around Pynchon's novels: "In its comic repetitions, manic zaniness and apocalypticism, as well as its metafiction, pop surrealism and undergirding paranoia, 'The Blow Out' dishes up a pretty decent map of the rhetoric we encounter in *The Crying of Lot 49* and *Gravity's Rainbow*. Whether we choose to read our *sacra pagina* in the Calvinist soteriology of preterite vs. elect, in Weber's economics of charisma vs. routine, or in binary metaphors derived from quantum physics, Pavlovian psychology, Christian gnosticism, or what-have-you doesn't make much difference" (56).

H91.29, B66.30 Filthy machine. As Slade points out, this is an appropriate judgment on the part of someone named after a god of speech and letters (138).

Berressem notes that "*Lot 49* follows the colonization and contamination of the subject's dreams via the *media*, especially television, which . . . not only *intrudes* into dreams, it actually *produces* and *simulates* them, in a feedback that ultimately conflates psychic and televised space" (85).

H91.33, B66.33 "The anarchist is dressed all in black." Like Driblette's Tristero assassins, whose aim appears to be the disruption of the kind of secure communication system that makes government possible.

H92.11, B67.3 supposed to burn bones Another component of the bone motif. This one, however, tends to muddy the waters. Here the agents of the Tristero are associated by implication both with Angelo, whose boneblack ink is the subject of gruesome and enigmatic punning in *The Courier's Tragedy* (H70.26), and with Pierce via the Beaconsfield filter experiments and the bones in the lake. The possible alternative to the oppressive forces of our culture is implicated in the dubious practices that give those forces their power, notwithstanding whatever sympathy vote may be won by Mr. Thoth's repeated disapproval of his grandfather's cruel delight in Indian killing.

H92.30, B67.20 trapped at the centre of some intricate crystal Just as she had felt with Driblette, and the spider's web threat of his eyes, so she feels trapped here by an imagined latticework of possibly threatening coincidences.

H92.31, B67.21 "My God." Further evidence, for some, of the novel's religious overtones. The conventional nature of this utterance suggests an appeal for help in the face of a possibly demonic threat. It is possible, however, to read this as a kind of intuitive identification on Oedipa's part of the sacred characteristics of the Tristero.

H93.24, B68.6 Probably hired by the Federal government. Fallopian's speculation brings with it the attendant association of the Tristero with some kind of covert governmental agency, something of a contradiction to the other, anarchistic, antiestablishment aspects of the organization's shadowy history.

H94.3, B68.12 one Genghis Cohen "In the *New York Times Book Review* of July 17, 1966, Pynchon has the following reply to Romain Gary, who charged that the name, 'Genghis Cohen,' found its way into *The Crying of Lot 49* from his own novel:

> I took the name Genghis Cohen from the name of Genghis Khan (1162–1227), the well-known Mongol warrior and statesman. If Mr. Gary really believes himself to be the only writer at present able to arrive at a play on words this trivial, that is another problem entirely, perhaps more psychiatric than literary, and I certainly hope he works it out. (22, 24)

What is especially interesting here is how willing Pynchon is to concede the triviality. He makes no statement of any great or distinctive purpose. He was merely being sportive, nothing more" (Caesar 10n).

H94.25, B68.39   room after room receding   "It is an appropriate spatial metaphor for the way the Tristero plot looms at the terminal point of endlessly receding possible interpretations" (Tanner, "V." 42).

"This vision comments metaphorically on the way texts and sources recede into each other apparently without end, stretching towards resolution but never reaching it" (Seed 127).

H94.28, B69.2   Barry Goldwater   The right-wing senator from Arizona who unsuccessfully ran for president in 1964.

H95.3, B69.9   signals like that   See Metzger on the subject of freeways and cemeteries (H61.9).

H95.5, B69.11   announcing his seizure   Accounts of the nature of the "aura" that precedes an attack vary widely, as the three possibilities (odor, color, grace note) suggest. The tone here does imply that the aura is more pleasant than otherwise, even though many descriptions indicate the contrary (Temkin 142).

H95.6, B69.12   this secular announcement   The fact that the announcement is described as "secular" of course implies that what is lost during the seizure is somehow sacred, tying in with the concept of revelation that has already become part of our understanding of the novel. Mendelson notes that "Pynchon's reference to epilepsy recalls its traditional status as a sacred disease" (113). That status goes back at least as far as 400 B.C.; the Hippocratic collection of sacred writings contains a book called *On the Sacred Disease*, in which a physician takes to task those who would attribute divine origin to epilepsy (Temkin 3).

Note, however, that Pynchon makes a distinction (between aura and actual seizure) that runs counter to other accounts of the possibly revelatory nature of the disease. Apparently some evidence exists linking the prophetic utterances of Mohammed with epilepsy, and another famous epileptic, Dostoyevski, picks up on this in his fiction, most notably in the person of Prince Myshkin in *The Idiot*. In that novel, Mohammed's vision of the abode of God is said to last in real time not long enough for a spilled jug of water to empty out, suggesting that the vision takes place in that split second before the actual seizure (quoted in Temkin 395). An acquaintance of Dostoyevski's recorded the following account of one of the novelist's own seizures one evening during his exile in Siberia: "At the same moment the bells of the neighboring church rang for Easter matins. The air was vibrant and full of sound. 'And I felt,' Feodor Mikhailovich [Dostoyevski] narrated, 'that heaven had come down to earth and had absorbed me. I really perceived God and was imbued with Him. Yes, God exists,—I cried,—and I do not remember any more' " (Temkin 373).

Finally, a description of Myshkin's preseizure experiences:

> In his epileptic condition there was one phase before the attack itself . . . when suddenly in the midst of sadness, mental darkness, oppression, his brain momentarily was as if set on fire, and all his vital forces strained themselves at once, in an unusual outburst. His consciousness and feeling of being alive became almost tenfold during these moments, which repeated themselves like lightning. His mind, his heart were illuminated with an unusual light; all excitement, all doubts, all troubles were at once as if at peace, solved in some higher calm full of clear harmonious joy and hope, full of intelligence and final reason. Yet these moments, these flashes were nothing but the presentiment of that final second (never more than a second) with which the attack itself started. This second was, of course, unbearable. (quoted in Temkin 394)

H95.11, B69.17 the central truth itself Oedipa is guided by the conventional assumption that reality is determinate, that there is, concerning any given set of circumstances, a "central truth" that will explain or account for most of what at first may seem mysterious. The idea that this truth might prove inaccessible, beyond her capacity to articulate it, is therefore threatening to her, particularly at this stage of her quest. The reader probably is governed by a similar assumption about the novel and may here be experiencing the first touches of the anxiety that will come to its fullest flowering on the last page of the novel, as it becomes clear that no "truth" is to be forthcoming.

H95.14, B69.19 destroying its own message irreversibly Oedipa will have a similar experience when she contemplates the loss of information that would be occasioned by the drunken sailor's self-immolation in his flophouse bed: "It was as if she had just discovered the irreversible process" (H128.24). The juxtaposition here of "message" and "irreversibly" anticipates the link between information theory and thermodynamics that will become explicit during Oedipa's visit to the home of John Nefastis (H105n). "Irreversibly" in this context seems to be equivalent to something nontechnical like "permanently" or "irrecoverably," while the later use in connection with the mattress is more obviously tied to physics.

H95.33, B69.36   the Pony Express issue   Issued on April 3, 1940, to commemorate the eightieth anniversary of the Pony Express, the stamp does indeed depict "a Pony Express rider galloping out of a western fort" (H97.18).

H96.10, B70.5   "What is this?"   "She is scared by the discovery of this shadow world which appears in filigree through her own world, of this other text described or pointed at in the underground letters travelling through WASTE" (Couturier 19).

H96.10, B70.5   wondering how much time had gone by   The implication is that Oedipa has once again experienced a kind of seizure, an absence, that has been heralded by the appearance of the WASTE symbol.

H96.17, B70.11   an old German stamp   Scott's 1895 catalog lists five likely candidates, issued by Thurn and Taxis in the Northern Postal District between 1852 and 1866, the year before Bismarck bought them out (see H96.23n). The ¼ represents a quarter of a silver groschen. One thaler would buy 120 such stamps.

H96.23, B70.17   until Bismarck bought them out   For the sum of three million thalers (Harlow 207).

H96.29, B70.23   "It was in their coat of arms."   Harlow reports that the Emperor Maximilian changed the armorial bearings of the Thurn and Taxis family in 1512, "adding thereto a golden horn of the coiled type which had begun to be carried by postriders to herald their approach at a station, or when meeting less important travelers on the road" (62).

H97.10, B70.36   obviously a counterfeit   The reader is unlikely to share Cohen's surprise at the obviousness of the "forgeries." He is thinking in terms of the possible economic benefits of counterfeiting, whereas, by now, we have become accustomed to thinking of the Tristero as being in some sense subversive in its intentions, rather than simply profit-oriented. The alterations to the stamps, therefore, are more in the vein of graffiti than anything else—the slogans scrawled on government buildings during protests spring to mind. Far from seeking to deceive, to conceal its own fraudulence, the defaced stamp offers itself in any number of ways as a mockery of the real stamp it so blatantly fails to imitate. The threat implicit in the feather (more powerfully felt by Oedipa than by Cohen, perhaps, by virtue of her conversation with Mr. Thoth) is repeated in the watermark rendition of the muted posthorn.

H98.6, B71.22 "what if it were as old as Thurn and Taxis?" Cohen's speculation turns out to be unfounded, since we later learn that the "founding figure" of the Tristero does not make his appearance until 1577 (H159.21).

H98.23, B71.39 suddenly in retreat Assuming that Oedipa is not simply imagining things, Cohen's behavior here is distinctly peculiar. His nervousness would seem to suggest greater knowledge of the Tristero than he is prepared to admit. At the same time, one has to wonder why he brings the stamps to Oedipa's attention at all if he is simply going to be frightened by the consequence. Perhaps the evidence Oedipa offers of the Tristero's continuing vitality rattles the essentially historically oriented Cohen, who may have had no idea that the "Adversary" could still be around to punish those who threaten it.

Of course, given the novel's overall tendency to resist certainty, we might be better advised simply to acknowledge this moment's unsettling quality, without anxiously seeking a rational explanation.

H99.1, B72.9 As if their home cemetery "This splendid passage combines almost all the book's central motifs: the alternate world 'where you could somehow walk,' the persistence of the world of the sacred present, the *tristesse* of the illumination that accompanies the Trystero" (Mendelson 134).

⌐◁ Chapter 5

H100.1,B73.1   her next move should have been   Why "should"?
What is the first-time reader to make of this somewhat cryptic suggestion of error on Oedipa's part? It creates the impression, surely,
that there is somehow a right way for Oedipa to be going about her
quest, and hence that there is a definite solution to the "problem"
of the Tristero.

   In retrospect, however, we see that the narrator is anticipating
the revelation of Driblette's death and the closing off of one avenue
of inquiry for Oedipa, though the implication that she might have
been able to prevent it is unsettling.

H100.7, B73.6   Metzger did not seem desperate   Far from it, as
it turns out (H147.24). Love does not fare well in the world of
Lot 49, falling victim to the solipsistic/narcissistic tendencies of
the male characters with whom Oedipa attempts to share herself
(H152.31n). Note, though, that Oedipa allows the mere mischance
of traffic flow and inattention to keep her from making contact
with Mucho.

H101.13, B74.5   a reproduction of a Remedios Varo   Cowart sur-
mises that the painting is possibly Varo's *Encuentro*, in which "a
woman opens one of a number of small caskets in a room, only to
find her own face staring back at her." He notes that the reference
to Varo is a reminder for Oedipa that everything she "discovers"
may be the product of her own imaginative weaving ("Varo" 24).

H101.24, B74.14   her own exhausted face   "The mirror may have
induced the dream. Oedipa looks as exhausted as if she had actually been making love. The suggestion is, clearly, that she has been
making love to herself in the mirror, like Narcissus" (Couturier
26). See also H41.23n for the Lacanian associations adduced by
some critics.

H101.34, B74.25   *No hallowed skein of stars*   Seed points out that
the variants Oedipa finds are a reminder that her desire for "textual
stability" will never be satisfied (123). It is also a salutary reminder
to the reader, one might add.

H102.20, B75.4 J.-K. Sale Probably a nod at Pynchon's Cornell friend, James Kirkpatrick Sale, a political journalist.

H103.16, B75.33 Wheeler Hall Home of the English department at Berkeley.

H103.21, B75.37 FSM's, YAF's, VDC's Political organizations with active memberships in the early sixties: Free Speech Movement, Young Americans for Freedom, Vietnam Day Committee. Both the FSM and the VDC were home-grown Berkeley organizations, markedly left-wing and antiestablishment in orientation. YAF, on the other hand, represented right-wing, anticommunist sentiments.

H103.24, B75.40 wanting to feel relevant Even at this stage, Oedipa is only beginning to sense her displacement from her deeply conventional past. The "nose-to-nose" dialogues of the students who populate this campus are indicative of the kind of intellectual exchange that can be achieved when prevailing norms have not become stultifying. Oedipa, however, is still unsure of her ability fully to accept an adversary relationship with her republic. Toward the end of the novel, she will come to see that only as an "alien, unfurrowed" could she be "relevant" to an America without a Tristero (H182.13).

H103.30, B76.6 certain pathologies in high places We can assume that Oedipa would have been in college in the mid to late fifties, at the height of the cold war. The death that was able to cure these pathologies was presumably Kennedy's.

H103.32, B76.8 Siwash According to the *New Dictionary of American Slang*, "Any small college; the archetypical small college." See H10.4n.

H104.8, B76.16 Secretaries James and Foster and Senator Joseph James Forrestal, Eisenhower's secretary of defense, John Foster Dulles, his secretary of state, and Joseph McCarthy. The three are linked by their strong anticommunist sentiments and hence by their sharing what looks in retrospect like the paranoia of cold war front-liners. Conroy identifies "James" as James Hagerty, Eisenhower's press secretary (60).

H104.13, B76.20 faceless pointsmen Pynchon will use this image to great advantage in the person of Edward Pointsman, the sad but sinister behaviorist in *Gravity's Rainbow*. Here he conjures up a disturbing vision of the faceless manipulators who shape the political destiny of the republic, portraying them as victims of their own cynicism.

Note, too, that one of James Clerk Maxwell's earliest descriptions of his famous demon was as a "pointsman for flying molecules" (letter to William Thomson, 1868, cited in Leff and Rex 39).

H104.16, B76.23   impossible to find ever again   Echoing the irreversible destruction of the revelatory message supposedly delivered during a seizure (H95.14n), and anticipating the "irreversible process" represented by the mattress (H128.25n). The world as Oedipa knew it is irrecoverable—the patterns of choices made and rejected are not reproducible from the observable consequences.

H104.25, B76.32   among the U.S. mailboxes   The unnecessary emphasis on "U.S." here serves as a reminder of the possible existence of other kinds of mailboxes.

H105.11, B77.10   He began then, bewilderingly   To which the reader, having struggled through Oedipa's attempt to reproduce Nefastis's explanation, might reasonably respond, "No kidding!" Such a response, I suppose, stems from a double difficulty, the first of which arises from our sharing Oedipa's inability to understand exactly what Nefastis means, and the second from the problem we might have in judging the relationship of his meaning to the novel as a whole—in one formulation, judging what Pynchon means. The notes that follow, then, represent an attempt to help the reader out of both these difficulties, first by elucidating the more esoteric aspects of Nefastis's account and second by offering a summary of at least some of the interpretive moves that have been made on the basis of that account.

Readers who wish to review the scientific debate sparked by Maxwell's hypothetical demon are referred to the collection of essays edited by Leff and Rex, in which a chronological bibliography affords an extremely useful overview.

H105.14, B77.13   two distinct kinds of this entropy   In his introduction to *Slow Learner*, Pynchon claims that he has been trying to understand the concept of entropy ever since he wrote his story of that name, but that his "grasp becomes less sure the more" he reads (14). No doubt the reader of *Lot 49* has reason to feel the same way. The experience of trying to grasp the full implications of the concept as it applies to Pynchon's novel is very much akin to that of the observer confronted with the optical indeterminacy of the open cube, which first presents one corner to the fore and then suddenly seems to have turned itself inside out. No claim is made, therefore, that the observations which follow resolve all the difficulties caused by this elusive metaphor. Like Oedipa, we are bound to remain uncertain, guided only, perhaps, by a few (not necessarily "gemlike") clues.

Entropy as it applies to thermodynamic systems is by no means a straightforward concept, and Nefastis has every reason to be "bothered" by the word. For our purposes, however, we can perhaps skirt some of the difficulties inherent in a full consideration of the topic by concentrating solely on the context in which it is raised here—that of Nefastis's Maxwell's demon machine.

Two approaches to the concept seem relevant, then, the first of which has the most obvious metaphorical reverberations. Common sense and the second law of thermodynamics tell us that, in the situation envisaged by Maxwell, the faster-moving molecules in the box would, in the absence of any intervention, gradually surrender energy to the slower ones until the total energy of the gas would be more or less randomly distributed throughout the box. At that point, the energy of the system would have been degraded to the point that it could not be used to do anything useful—to drive a piston, for example—and we would say that the system's entropy was at a maximum. "The usefulness of thermal energy derives from order—specifically, from the orderly division of heat and cold into distinct regions. Without such temperature variation there would be no relatively cold regions for the heat to pass to, and it is only during such passage that heat can be harnessed" (Engel 51). Any process that brings about an ordering of the system thus brings about a reduction in entropy, and this is of course what the demon is supposedly capable of doing.

From this point of view, therefore, we can say that entropy measures the availability of the energy in a system to do useful work. It is clear that Pynchon's earliest understanding of the concept falls in line with this definition and is influenced in part by the work of Norbert Wiener, who notes that, "as entropy increases, the universe, and all closed systems in the universe, tend naturally to deteriorate and lose their distinctiveness, to move from the least to the most probable state, from a state of organization and differentiation in which distinctions and forms exist, to a state of chaos and sameness" (quoted in Abernethy 20). As Abernethy points out, a very similar view is attributed to Callisto, in Pynchon's story "Entropy":

> "Nevertheless," continued Callisto, "he found in entropy, or the measure of disorganization for a closed system, an adequate metaphor to apply to certain phenomena in his own world. He saw, for example, the younger generation responding to Madison Avenue with the same spleen his own had once reserved for Wall Street, and in American 'consumerism' discovered a similar tendency from the least to the most probable, from differentiation to sameness, from ordered individuality to a kind of chaos. He . . . envisioned a heat-death for his culture in which ideas, like heat-energy, would no longer be transferred, since each point in it would ultimately have the same quantity of energy; and intellectual motion would, accordingly, cease." (quoted in Abernethy 23)

Pynchon continues to exploit this aspect of the concept of entropy in *Lot 49*—for example, in the image of the "unvarying gray sickness" that Mucho envisages (H14.24n)—but he also brings into play the issue of probability that Wiener mentions, thus paving the way for the introduction of meanings drawn from the field of information theory. In this approach to entropy, instead of describing the system in terms of the availability or usefulness of its energy, we would view entropy as the measure of the likelihood of the system's arriving at the state in which we find it at any given moment. The appropriate formulation of the second law, therefore, would be something like the following: "A closed system will always end up in that condition which can be realized in the greatest number of ways" (Bolton 200). A high degree of entropy, then, is associated with a high degree of probability, or, to put it another way, the more likely a given state of a system is to occur, the more entropic the system is. The random distribution of heat throughout the water in a bathtub, for example, is a much more likely occurrence over time than the concentration of heat in one corner, simply because there are many more possible arrangements of the individual water molecules that would bring about the former state of affairs than would result in the latter. In the case of Nefastis's machine, the demon's sorting activities bring the system into a state of order whose unlikeliness is related to the limited number of ways of arriving at such a configuration when no external agency is involved. By introducing order, the demon is bucking the odds in a big way.

The particular order that the demon brings into being is readily described in terms of the location of individual molecules before and after the sorting process. Before the demon makes its measurements, each of the molecules has the freedom to be anywhere in the box, and hence what Gatlin calls the "configurational variety" of the system is very high (30). After the demon makes its measurement, molecules whose energy exceeds the mean energy of the gas will be confined to one half of the box, while molecules whose energy is lower than the mean will be confined to the other half of the box. As a result, our ability to locate a given molecule has increased by 50 percent, and hence our degree of certainty about the system has also increased. With lowered entropy comes greater certainty.

Readers who are familiar with the many discussions of this aspect of the novel will recognize the confusion that can be introduced by the adoption of a slightly different conceptual perspective. The association postulated above, for example, seems to be radically at odds with Tanner's claim that *increase* in entropy results in increase in certainty ("Crying" 184). The contradiction results from Tanner's choosing to think of a system in terms of the macroscopic ensemble of its individual microstates, and hence to associate "certainty" with the degree of probability that a *generalized* description of the system in question will be accurate.

From this point of view, an increase in entropy is indeed accompanied by an increase in certainty—we can be more certain that our description of a highly entropic system will be accurate because the number of statistically plausible macroscopic configurations of that system is very small. In the case of the bathtub, then, we can be almost 100 percent certain that the water will not vary significantly in temperature from one region of the bathtub to another. The probability that we would find one corner of the bathtub filled with hot water, while not zero, is extremely low. I think that, on balance, it is probably more helpful to think of entropy as related directly to *uncertainty*, particularly since we are concerned with the behavior of a demon which can sort individual molecules, and also because that approach affords easier access to the link with information theory that the novel forges.

With these two definitions of entropy in mind, we can now turn to the question of whether Nefastis in fact believes that his machine can bring about a net decrease in entropy, an assumption that most critics seem to make. When Oedipa innocently objects to Koteks's claim that the demon does no work by asking, "Sorting isn't work?" (H86.19), she anticipates Nefastis's own articulation of the same objection: "But somehow the loss [of entropy] was offset by the information the Demon gained about what molecules were where." I think that Nefastis has attempted to explain to Oedipa (without much success) something resembling the major objection to Maxwell's hypothesis that was current when Pynchon was writing *Lot 49*. In brief, physicists argued that the acquisition of information (more accurately, the reduction of informational uncertainty) by measurement cannot be thought of as cost-free. In order to determine the speed of each molecule, the claim went, the demon must employ some kind of perception involving light of a frequency different from that of the blackbody radiation that quantum theory insists would be flooding the interior of the box. The demon "sees" the molecule in the light reflected from it, but the light energy is dissipated into heat in the process, bringing about an increase in entropy at least as great as the decrease accomplished as a result of the knowledge the demon gains about the molecule. It is reasonable to say that an increase in certainty on the part of the demon about the characteristics of each molecule allows for a decrease in the entropy of the system, but that decrease is "offset" by the actual process of acquiring the necessary knowledge. Nefastis seems to be aware that the demon alone is not capable of violating the second law.

Further evidence is afforded when Nefastis speaks of "all that massive complex of information, destroyed over and over with each power stroke" (H106.1). I think it is not immediately clear what he means by the destruction of information here, but I believe that speculations by researchers interested in the physics of computation, which were first voiced in the early sixties, are potentially helpful. Landauer, for example, suggested as early as 1961 that it is not so much in the acquisition of information about the behavior of each molecule that an increase in entropy occurs as in the necessity for the demon to *discard* information in order to make room for the next piece of data. Landauer's work has since been cited and expanded by a number of other theorists, among them C. H. Bennett, who offers the following account of Landauer's argument:

> Landauer's proof begins with the premise that distinct logical states of a computer must be represented by distinct physical states of the computer's hardware. For example, every possible state of the computer's memory must be represented by a distinct physical configuration (that is, a distinct set of currents, voltages, fields, and so forth).
>
> Suppose a memory register of n bits is cleared; in other words, suppose the value in each location is set at zero, regardless of the previous value. Before the operation the register as a whole could have been in any of 2^n states. After the operation the register can be in only one state. The operation has therefore compressed many logical states into one, much as a piston might compress a gas.
>
> By Landauer's premise, in order to compress a computer's logical state, one must also compress its physical state: one must lower the entropy of its hardware. According to the second law, this decrease in the entropy of the computer's hardware cannot be accomplished without a compensating increase in the entropy of the computer's environment.

Hence one cannot clear a memory register without generating heat and adding to the entropy of the environment (116).

If we can grant that the demon in Nefastis's machine resembles a computer, and if we assume that it does not have an infinitely large memory, we can see that it must periodically discard its knowledge about the molecules in order to make room for subsequent measurements. I take the clearing of the demon's memory to be equivalent to the destruction of information that Nefastis mentions.

This all seems to me to suggest that Nefastis knows his power source, the sensitive, is not an integral part of a closed system machine, but instead is an external energy reservoir that in turn needs to take in energy in order to function. Schaub appears to recognize that this *ought* to be the case—"the Demon requires some input from the Outside to 'keep it all cycling'—this is, I take it, Oedipa's purpose as a 'sensitive'" ("Open Letter" 94)—although he claims that Nefastis's account "doesn't actually match" the model. Regardless of the difficulties involved in conceiving of information as exactly equivalent to energy, we can see that Nefastis is in a sense keeping company with a long line of inventors who have sought alternative forms of energy.

If thermodynamics and statistical mechanics were the only sources of Nefastis's inspiration, we might have some hope of coming away with a coherent understanding of his invention. The introduction of information theory, however, complicates the issue considerably. Just as with its thermodynamic counterpart, information entropy has spawned a wide variety of definitions. As was noted earlier, the most useful of these connect information with uncertainty and hence with thermodynamic entropy.

Before proceeding with this difficult topic, however, a word of caution is in order. The word "information" in this context cannot be thought of in its usual sense as being equivalent to some specific meaning encoded in language or numbers, or symbols of some other kind. In the words of one of the early theorists in the field: "This word 'information' in communication theory relates not so much to what you do say, as to what you could say" (Weaver, quoted in Gatlin 48). When theorists refer to quantities of information, they are therefore indicating the capacity of a transmission system to transmit meaning, not to something that might loosely be called an "amount of meaning," which would anyway be a nebulous concept. Information and meaning are in fact mutually exclusive of one another, in that meaning emerges only when choices are made from among sets of symbols—only, that is, as the majority of available information is rejected through some selection process. By writing the word "cat," for example, I reject all the other words available to me in English, annihilating, if only temporarily, all the information represented by the rest of the English lexicon. When Nefastis speaks of "the information the Demon gained about what molecules were where," then he is using the word in its ordinary sense, meaning "knowledge," not in its communication theory sense, as I think some critics, notably Palmeri and Schaub, have supposed.

It has become a commonplace of commentary on the novel that the relevant source for the information theory aspect of Nefastis's machine is the work of Claude Shannon, who seems to have been the first explicitly to associate information with entropy and to link both with the concept of uncertainty. The tendency to focus on Shannon is understandable, given Nefastis's explicit reference to the two kinds of entropy, but the situation is complicated by the fact that he clearly associates the congruence of the equations for the two entropies with work done in "the 30's." Shannon's findings were first published not in the thirties but in 1948. Mangel, whose article is the one most often cited in this context, reproduces Boltzmann's equation for thermodynamic entropy and Shannon's for "average information-per-symbol," revealing that indeed the two are "precisely the same," but in no way accounting for the discrepancy in the dates (202). Subsequent commentary has followed Mangel's lead.

Either Nefastis (or Pynchon) has got his dates wrong, or we have to look for equations other than Shannon's that forge a link between "heat engines" and "communication." Shannon himself provides some guidance here when he acknowledges his debt to the work of R. V. L. Hartley, who published the paper "Transmission of Information" in the *Bell System Technical Journal* in 1928. In that paper, Hartley seeks to define a quantitative measure of information, and arrives at the conclusion that "the logarithm of the number of possible symbol sequences" constitutes such a measure. Where H is the "amount of information," n is the number of selections made from among s, the number of symbols available at each selection, Hartley then concludes: $H = n \log s$ (540). "If we put n equal to unity," Hartley continues, "we see that the information associated with a single selection is the logarithm of the number of symbols available" (541). In a situation where $s = 2$ (a binary choice, for example), $H = \log 2$. Hartley's definition very closely resembles another of Boltzmann's equations for thermodynamic entropy: $S = K \log W$, where W is the number of possible microstates of the system and K is an arbitrary constant. It also coincides very well with Leo Szilard's 1929 finding that "the mean value of the quantity of entropy produced by a measurement is $S = k \log 2$" (127). The measurement that Szilard refers to is a binary one—an indication of whether a piston should be moved up or down. Given this juxtaposition, it is hard not to conclude that $H = S$, or that "entropy" and "amount of information" are, or can sometimes be regarded as, equivalent. When Hartley's s is large—when there is a large number of possible symbols to choose from at each selection—then his H is also large. Amount of information is directly proportional to the number of possibilities available in a given transmission system before a message is transmitted. When the demon makes a measurement, the information content of the system composed of the demon and the molecule is in fact reduced, since the demon now knows whether the molecule possesses either $<x$ or $>x$ units of energy, where x is the mean kinetic energy of the gas molecules in the box. This reduction is transmitted to the system as a whole by the demon's manipulation of the gate, which results in the confinement of each of the molecules to only half of the available volume of the box. This confinement, which lowers the entropy of the system, also lowers its information content by reducing uncertainty about the location of each of the molecules.

Nefastis says that the congruence between Hartley's formula and the Boltzmann/Szilard entropy equation is merely coincidental, except in the case of Maxwell's demon, where, he claims, a mathematical analogy becomes an objective truth. Leaving aside the fact that physicists in fact seem more likely than not to assert the physical connectedness of information and entropy, we must now attempt to follow the final conceptual leap that allows Nefastis to connect his machine to its power source, the sensitive.

Among the various difficulties faced by the demon in the performance of its appointed task, perhaps the most relevant for our purposes is that posed by thermal fluctuation. Because the demon is part of the system it inhabits, it is vulnerable to disturbances resulting from collisions with gas molecules and photons from blackbody radiation. These disturbances are likely to be compounded by the heat/information it absorbs from the measurements it performs (Leff and Rex 11). "If we assume that the specific heat of the demon is not infinite, it must heat up. It has but a finite number of internal gears and wheels, so it cannot get rid of the extra heat. . . . Soon it is shaking from Brownian motion so much that it cannot tell whether it is coming or going, much less whether the molecules are coming or going, so it does not work" (Richard Feynman, quoted in Leff and Rex 11). The implication of this is clear: "If a demon heats up, periodic dumping of energy to an external reservoir is needed to keep its temperature approximately equal to the temperature of the gas in which it resides. . . . Of course, feeding entropy to the reservoir helps to keep the second law intact" (Leff and Rex 11).

In order to perform in a cyclical fashion, the demon must periodically be returned to its initial state—one in which it is once again capable of performing its measurements accurately. The demon, in other words, must be "reset." This is surely the process that Nefastis is describing when he says that "the sensitive must receive that staggering set of energies, and feed back something like the same quantity of information." The "staggering set of ener-

gies" is the thermodynamic result of the acquisition of information by the demon. As we have already seen, the demon acts as a
measuring device of the kind described by Szilard. Each measure-
ment the demon makes generates an entropy equivalent to $k \log 2$, so the total entropy per cycle would be that amount multiplied
by the number of measurements—the number of molecules in the
box. (We have already noted that this amount can be regarded as
equivalent to the amount of "data" the demon has accumulated,
via the congruence of Hartley's quantitative measure and Szilard's
"entropy cost" calculation. Perhaps the slight difficulty inherent
in Nefastis's remark about passing on data is removed by this association). Because the entropy of the gas itself is reduced by the
demon's sorting activities, the entropy increase must be located
in the demon itself. If the system were indeed a closed one, the
massive increase in the demon's entropy each cycle would soon
render it incapable of performing its task unless it could channel
the entropy to an outside "dump," or "garbage can."

But the entropy that the demon dumps represents degraded
energy—energy drawn from the system by the process of observation and dissipation. In order for the system to "keep cycling," an
equivalent amount of nondegraded energy must be returned to the
demon (Leff and Rex 13–14). Here we run into a very easily per-
ceivable difficulty—one that has been advanced by physicists uneasy with the subjectivist implications of attempts to link thermodynamics and information theory. "In general it seems difficult
to conceive of many situations in which 'information' . . . can be
made use of by humans, or by automata, for the purpose of seizing
hold of the momentary fluctuations which occur within physico-
chemical systems. Of course it must be accepted that the Second
Law is a statistical law, and is only true on the average. Therefore
it would not be really shocking (only very, very surprising) if we
did sometimes succeed in trapping such systems in slightly low
entropy states. On the other hand it would be exceedingly shocking, as well as surprising, if a sequence of symbols on a piece of
paper, or inscribed on a magnetic tape, or held in someone's head,
were ever capable of being the *cause* of such an event" (Denbigh,

"Subjective" 114). Nefastis, however, clearly conceives of information as a kind of energy, presumably on the basis of the "objectively true" relationship between information and entropy that the Maxwell's demon situation permits. He is not alone in making the connection. Wiener, for example, acknowledges that "there is no sharp boundary between energetic coupling and informational coupling" (37). Also, speculations in the early sixties on the subject of information processing by computers suggested a connection between logical processes and the physical constraints associated with them. Nefastis's belief in the capacity of a sensitive to communicate with the demon is enough to indicate his assumption of a physical channel through which a certain amount of energy in the form of "information" can be sent to the demon, restoring it to a state in which it is capable of performing a new set of measurements. "Information" here seems to be a physical equivalent of "capacity to process knowledge," a sense that is not too distant from its usage in the field of communication. The sensitive gauges the "quantity of information" necessary from the "data" that the demon has passed on to her—a simple enough calculation, given the equivalence of Hartley's and Szilard's equations.

For the most part, critics have not been very flattering in their judgment of John Nefastis. Mendelson thinks his science is "unbalanced," and regards "the whole effect" of Nefastis's description of his machine as "one of Blavatskian mumbo-jumbo" (126, 129). Tanner dismisses Nefastis as "a lunatic" who believes in "a crazy fantasy of his own making" ("Crying" 184). We have already noted glosses on his name (H85.30n). Palmeri also rather unkindly suggests that Nefastis's crewcut and Polynesian shirt identify him immediately as "an unmistakable science nerd" (982). Certainly the engineer's references to "young stuff" and the inappropriate assumption that Oedipa is sexually available do not imply a highly evolved consciousness.

As a result of these negative connotations, there is a tendency for critics to want to dismiss Nefastis and his invention as sources of positive meaning in the novel. Nicholson, for example, noting the relationship between disorder and information, claims that

"Nefastis's attempt through Maxwell's demon to extract mechanical energy by reducing a disorderly system to order, is anti-entropic in the Information Theory sense, therefore anti-communicative, negative. . . . It is precisely because he is willing to exchange information for power that Nefastis is unspeakable to the gods; his machine swaps communication for stultifying order" (102). This view fails to acknowledge that maximum entropy of information, the equivalent of a high degree of uncertainty, corresponds with unintelligibility. Real communication takes place only when a balance is achieved between order and disorder. The cycle of communication that is set up between the demon and the sensitive is designed to maintain such a balance and to keep the system cycling while performing useful work. To regard this as "stultifying" seems odd.

Hayles argues from a similar perspective in her recent essay on the novel, where she claims that, "several years before he wrote *The Crying of Lot 49*, Pynchon had already sensed that disorder, conceived as maximum information rather than dissipation, could offer an exit from the traditional 'exitlessness' of heat death scenarios" (112). Like Abernethy, though in the service of a somewhat different argument, Hayles sees Nefastis's machine as "demonic," in that it "destroys information to create a trivial mechanical movement" (112).

Eddins also relies on the religious connotations of the demon in his negative reading of the machine's implications: "In the world of *Lot 49* . . . there is only the spurious gnostic Demon, a man-made (or, at least, man-conceived) entity designed to interfere—through a kind of magic—with natural process. Insofar as this intervention defeats the generalized Death immanent in heat-death, it obviously has a normative function; but this function is compromised, as are all gnostic 'positives,' by antinatural means and demonic provenance" (100).

Other readings leave aside the question of the credibility of the machine or its inventor, relying instead on the suggestive nature of the concepts that are brought into play. Kharpertian's position is fairly typical: "The concept of entropy serves Pynchon as the metaphor for Oedipa's quest of the Tristero. In thermodynamic terms, Oedipa moves from a state of greater entropy, a condition of inactive uniformity in which her 'days seemed . . . more or less identical,' to a state of lesser entropy, a condition of active diversity made possible by the apparent existence of the Tristero. In cybernetic terms, however, she moves in the opposite direction, that is, from lesser to greater entropy, as the multiplicity of information she gathers about the Tristero increases the uncertainty of the information's ultimate significance" (104). Mendelson, who does judge Nefastis, expresses a similar view: "In *The Crying of Lot 49* Oedipa receives more and more surprises, more and more rapidly, and entropy . . . increases—but . . . it is information entropy rather than thermodynamic entropy, and the effect of the increase is invigorating rather than stagnating" (128). Mendelson later gave ground on the more positive aspects of this reading in the face of Schaub's insistence that "Mendelson is too happy" ("Open Letter" 94). Schaub says that he wishes "only to assert the ominous, paralytic aspect of [the] information increase" in which Mendelson finds comfort.

In the light of these more or less negative approaches to Nefastis and his machine, we might want to go back for a moment to the first mention of the engineer, which seems to suggest that there is at least some reason to regard him in a sympathetic light. "John's somebody who still invents things," Stanley Koteks tells Oedipa, indicating that Nefastis is to be counted among those "really creative engineer[s]" who would be stifled by the patent-grabbing policies of Yoyodyne (H85.14). In a world where originality, uniqueness, and difference are likely to be the only means of salvation in the face of an increasing tendency toward uniformity, such a person is surely someone to be valued. Perhaps the gods to whom Nefastis is "unspeakable" are in fact the gods of corporate America, the stultifying powers whose monopolistic control of the means of communication is one of the novel's prime targets.

In fact, one of the most frequently repeated interpretive moves involving Nefastis's invention may help us to see it as a more positive figurative device. Mangel was among the earliest of those who assert a symbolic connection between Oedipa and the demon:

"Just as the Demon, by sorting the molecules, gains information about them, so Oedipa shuffles through countless people and places, gathering information about the elusive Trystero" (197). The importance of this association lies in its implicit recognition that Oedipa, like the demon, needs to receive some form of energy from outside herself if she is to escape the confines of her tower. The revelations that seem to be about to burst through to her constitute a potential source of energy, "intrusions into this world from another," in the words of Jesús Arrabal, the exiled anarchist (H124.23). The cycling machine, with its seemingly miraculous openness to the flow of information from outside, thus constitutes an image of some power as Oedipa learns the danger of closed systems, and as she grows to understand the significance of Pierce's advice to "keep it bouncing" (H178.30n).

Although Oedipa is unable to confirm that the machine is anything other than the hallucination of a "sincere nut," she is not as dismissive of Nefastis as some readers. Her skepticism is in part the product of her fear: "In her colon now she was afraid, growing more so, that nothing would happen." She feels that there is something potentially "wonderful" in Nefastis's belief in his machine, just as she will envy the drunken sailor his glimpse of "worlds no other man had seen" (H129.22). Her sense of distress at the inaccessibility of the information coded in the mattress is anticipated here as she senses her inability to tap into a potentially huge energy source in her own brain.

H106.31, B78.20 two Yogi Bears . . . Peter Potamus Yogi Bear cartoons had been running since 1958, but Magilla Gorilla and Peter Potamus cartoons were syndicated in 1964 and were thus new to the TV screen.

H108.1, B79.14 "Have sexual intercourse" "Both sex and spirituality for [Nefastis] require the mediation of a communication device" (Slade 164).

H108.17, B79.29 heading irreversibly for the Bay Bridge Oedipa is caught up in the flow, not just of the rush-hour traffic, but also of time, whose arrow points inexorably and irreversibly to the future. She has just been introduced to some of the complexities of the concept of entropy, which is intimately linked with the idea of the irreversibility of actual physical processes.

H108.27, B79.38   Amid the exhaust, sweat, glare . . . freeway   The regularity of the calm pool surface and of the streets of San Narciso reflects an ordering process that has gone too far, producing a numbing effect that suppresses brain activity by depriving the mind of variety. The freeway, which is not completely disorganized, but which does evince a degree of chaotic vitality, provides a more stimulating and therefore thought-provoking environment.

H109.1, B80.5   (to take a recent example)   This is puzzling. A recent example of what?

H109.3, B80.7   say by coincidence   Interestingly enough, Oedipa is not as ready as Nefastis to regard the connection between thermodynamic and information entropy as coincidental. She simply admits that this is what Nefastis thinks. The more important issue for her is the way in which Nefastis appears to have transformed coincidence into something more structured. She seems no longer troubled by the possibility she had raised earlier (H106.10) that the structuring power of the demon may be simply the product of the coincidence itself.

H109.7, B80.10   a metaphor of God knew how many parts   Hayles uses this as the title of her recent essay on *Lot 49*, in which she argues that the novel is driven by "a two-cycle engine, whose motive power derives from the differential between the concrete and abstract polarities within metaphor" (101). She argues that the Tristero itself is constructed out of both poles of the metaphoric, the concrete and the abstract, appearing at different times to be one rather than the other but never finally resolving itself into either.

H109.10, B80.3   nothing but a sound . . . to hold them together   We have seen that Oedipa envies Nefastis the vision afforded him by his belief in the demon. She would clearly like to find something that would enable her to believe in the Tristero as a way of holding together all the coincidences that have been crowding in on her.

H109.25, B80.26   Either Trystero did exist   The first inkling of the binary choices that will come to seem so burdensome to Oedipa.

H109.30, B80.31   She had only to drift   "But if she did give in and drift at random—like Mucho with his drugs, Hilarius with his paranoia, Metzger with his opportunism, Jesús Arrabal with his political persistence, or the dropouts who rebel against the system that may be co-opting them—if she did give up her purposeful pursuit, she would become part of the cast of aimless caricatures that form the novel's ground" (Pearce 223).

H110.1, B80.34   North Beach   Home to the City Lights bookstore and such "beat" luminaries as Lawrence Ferlinghetti.

H110.6, B81.1   Roos Atkins suits   Suits sold by a San Francisco retail clothing center headed by Robert Roos.

H110.12, B81.7   Arnold Snarb   According to Couturier, "This is more than a convenient way to open a conversation with the IA; she is acknowledging the fact that she has turned into a man in San Francisco among all the homosexuals" (24).

H110.33, B81.27   "Finocchio's"   A San Francisco club famous for its drag shows.

H111.10, B81.37   She should have left then   Once again Pynchon introduces an oddly unfocused point of view. This seems to be Oedipa's opinion, but it is hard to know how far ahead we need to read before we discover exactly why she "should have left" the bar. If she had left at this moment she would probably have never known about the IA, but this would scarcely have been to her advantage. Certainly, learning about the IA affords her very little in the way of threatening or unpleasant information—in fact the visit to the Greek Way seems designed mainly to give Pynchon the opportunity to indulge in a flight of comic fantasy. There's a kind of fake or unjustified portentousness to the "should" here.

H111.33, B82.19   "I use the U.S. Mail"   Oedipa here seems to acknowledge her understanding of the revolutionary implications of the Tristero and of the possibility that the shadowy organization might in fact represent some positive alternative to the confining structures of the government's communications monopoly. It is possible, of course, that she is being disingenuous in an effort to elicit information.

H112.28, B83.6   "Inamorati Anonymous"   Bennet notes the antisocial nature of the IA, arguing that it "burlesques Oedipa's fantasy that it is possible to be simultaneously outside and inside society" (37). The fact that the WASTE system is being used in at least one instance to *prevent* the formation of human ties makes it hard to view the Tristero unequivocally as the representative of antisolipsistic, inclusive impulses in contemporary culture. Palmeri sees the IA as an instance of the novel's concern with narcissism, noting that "almost all the men Oedipa encounters abandon her and retreat into a self-contained state of fascination with themselves" (986). The fact is that, as Hayles points out, "the values assigned to the Tristero keep changing—sometimes menacing, sometimes comforting; sometimes metaphysical abstraction, sometimes historical conspiracy; sometimes illusory, sometimes real" (121). Hayles sees this as a model of the "profoundly ambiguous relationship of the text to its own language."

H113.7, B83.12 "We're isolates" Deliberately seeking the encapsulation that Oedipa is in the process of escaping as best she can.

H114.8, B84.10 The Stack There are those who maintain that this is a reference to a "stack" of interleaved freeway flyovers in downtown L.A. Others note that the Capital Records building resembles a stack of records, though the occupants of that building deny that it has ever been called "The Stack."

H114.20, B84.21 his Brody The expression to take (or pull) a Brody derives from the exploits of Steve Brodie, who is reputed to have jumped from the Manhattan side of the Brooklyn Bridge on July 23, 1886, to win a two-hundred-dollar bet. The sense of the expression is thus to take a suicidal leap.

H114.33, B84.32 Normany hedgerows Presumably a misprint for Normandy, where the D-Day invasion forces landed in World War II.

H115.4, B84.37 an IBM 7094 Top of the line in the early sixties, this computer used transistors rather than the bulky vacuum tubes of earlier models. The 7094 made time-sharing possible, allowing several terminals to be connected to the mainframe, each at full power.

H115.32, B85.23 "A sign" This is consistent with the associations that have already been established between the Tristero and the idea of revelation. The comic tone of this whole incident, however, coupled with the previously noted solipsistic characteristics of the IA, should warn us that too slavish a devotion to any one interpretive schema can be shown to have its weakness.

H116.2, B85.25 "My big mistake was love." Despite the persistently comic tone of this account, the degree of alienation from commonly accepted standards of human warmth and connectedness that it implies is chilling and may well come back to haunt us when we leave Oedipa at the end of the novel, shut up with the cruel-faced men in mohair suits.

H116.26, B86.8   any sexual relevance Oedipa's situation in the bar foreshadows her later concern with the larger issue of her "relevance" to America as a whole. Her sexual isolation translates into the paranoid isolation that may turn out to be "the only way she could continue, and manage to be at all relevant to [America]" (H182.11n).

H117.1, B86.16   the infected city "An extraordinary phrase, one charged with such meaning we must almost imagine Dante amongst the damned" (Merrill 61). In fact, it is the tone of the phrase, rather than its actual meaning, that strikes Merrill so forcibly. Just what the phrase does mean may be hard to determine. Possibly plague-stricken Thebes is being invoked. Oedipa perhaps, in retrospect, sees the city as "infected" by the ubiquitous presence of the post horn symbol, much as one might note the symptoms of a disease on the body of the sufferer. In this light, the Tristero has to be regarded as the disease itself, a reading that is reinforced by Oedipa's conclusion that she was being "beat up on" by "this malignant, deliberate replication" (H124.13). Dugdale, however, sees Oedipa's rhetoric as "self-persuasive," arguing that Oedipa is seeking the means to bring unity to a world that seems to be disintegrating—"the repetition of symbols is really the something which protects her from trauma" (133).

More straightforwardly, we might see the infection's symptoms in the "madness, perversion, despair and all manner of outsiders and disaffected subcultures" that she encounters during her journey through the city (Dugdale 133).

HII7.3, B86.I7 spent the rest of the night Noting that Oedipa "has become attenuated into disembodied eyes and ears," Seed reads the night's experiences positively, regarding them as potentially "exhilarating" in contrast to the "fear" that usually charges Oedipa's isolation (134). Hite appears to share this view: "Her long dark night, the central event of the novel, represents a radical enlargement of her vision. Significantly, it is the episode in the book that is most conspicuously free of parody" (87). Prasanta Das suggests that Oedipa's experience inverts the normal pattern of the American "night journey" (as typified in "Young Goodman Brown" and *The Narrative of Arthur Gordon Pym*), since the journey is an attempt to confirm an *external* reality rather than a projection of some inner state (5).

HII7.II, B86.25 a man, perhaps a man This shadowy figure, of indeterminate gender, who may or may not be dressed as a priest, is strongly reminiscent of the Bad Priest in *V.*

HII7.2I, B86.33 Later, possibly Obviously a great deal can be made of the implicit undermining of the accuracy of Oedipa's perceptions achieved in this sentence. Dugdale, for example, cites the passage as evidence of the fact that "Oedipa's revelations are overtly brought into doubt" (133), while Nicholson makes a familiar connection when he asserts that "the reader, too, feels a comparable uncertainty in the task of sorting the novel into real or imagined" (97). These are not unreasonable conclusions, but they do not take into account the complication introduced by the word "possibly." The fact is that we have no indication that Oedipa actually *did* at some point have difficulty sorting out the real from the imagined; we have only her (implied) acknowledgment that events as bizarre as those she witnesses *might* later come to seem less firmly rooted in the actual. There is an unspoken extension to the sentence: "Later, possibly, she would . . . ," but for now she was seeing what she was seeing. Memory might prove unreliable ("perhaps she did not see it as often as she later was to remember seeing it" [H123.32n]), but the account we are given of her discoveries seems scarcely mediated by the uncertainties of recollection—only once does she *think* she sees the symbol, the rest of the time she "saw," or "found" it, without any ambiguity in the telling.

H117.27, B86.40 customary words and images The language of the guide books, cosmeticizing the city. This brief aside recalls the extended commentary on tourism as a way of seeing afforded in *V.* by repeated references to Baedeker land. The phrase "for all but tourists to see" generates a similar resonance, though an oddly contradictory note is struck by the placing of the eyesores of the city "out on the skin," since it is precisely the inability of tourism to get beneath the surface of a place that is indicted in the earlier novel.

H118.3, B87.8 *She was meant to remember.* Further indication of Oedipa's readiness to accept that she may be the target of an organized plot. The potentially dangerous aspect of the Tristero is more than hinted at in the passage that follows. The possibility that she has been deliberately exposed to evidence of the Tristero's existence holds a deadly fascination for Oedipa. The "voluptuous field" harks back to the "languid sinister blooming" that earlier described the process of initiation Oedipa is undergoing (H54.13). There is something almost sexual in the tone of this passage, hinting at a sexuality whose darkest side surfaces in the activities of the Alameda County Death Cult, whose number Oedipa does not copy down (H122.29n).

Tyson reads Oedipa's fascination as symptomatic of her desire for a kind of "psychological death, the release from existential contingency and responsibility, that results from believing that all that occurs is meant to occur; that she, like everything else, is merely fulfilling a purpose imposed from the outside; that she is not responsible. . . the release from existential subjectivity, not sex, is the big turn-on" (15).

H118.16, B87.20 the direct, epileptic Word The immediate reference is back to Oedipa's earlier comparison of her sensitivity to "signals" to the aura of the epileptic (H95.3n). The Word, then, is presumably equivalent to "what is revealed during the attack," the nonsecular insight that the epileptic can never remember. The capitalization makes direct reference to scripture, and hence to the whole tradition of exegesis focusing on the "Logos" that Stimpson brings into play: "Pynchon may be going on to give 'the Word' special meaning. Some theoreticians of Logos—the Stoics, the Jewish philosopher Philo, the early Christian apologist Justin Martyr—thought of the divine principle as germinating, seminal, the '*spermatikos logos.*' Justin writes of 'the seed of reason . . . implanted in every race of man.' He mentions the 'spermatic word.' The Tristero may be delivering it. Pynchon, exploiting the puns natural language is heir to, literalizing a sexual metaphor, may want us to think of mail as male. If so, as Oedipa succumbs to the languid, sinister attraction of the Tristero, she represents the female body being pierced and receiving some sacred seed" (44). This is consistent with the views of a number of other critics who, developing the Marian associations that appear to accrete around Oedipa, argue for the relevance of the Annunciation as well as Pentecost to a reading of the novel.

Tanner notes that the clues, with their potential for infinite replication, offer scant compensation for the loss of the "singular" Word: "The 'cry' that might have ended the night is replaced by a 'crying' that can only extend it" ("Crying" 181). The "night" that would be abolished by the Word is unspecified; it could represent Oedipa's confinement in the tower of herself, or it could more generally represent the darkness of the marginal condition imposed by our culture on so many of its members—those for whom the Tristero is perhaps a champion.

H118.29, B87.32   their own unpenetrated sense of community   We are reminded that the various groups and individuals associated with the Tristero via the post horn symbol do not themselves stand out as representatives of the openness and cross-boundary information exchange that the novel as a whole appears to favor. The "piercing" that Oedipa undergoes by virtue of her exposure to these "clues" in essence grants her an insight that few of those she observes are capable of achieving. Her situation is oddly akin to that of the unfortunate Mr. Quistgard, in Donald Barthelme's *Snow White*, who receives a letter from a complete stranger, telling him that "even a plenum . . . can be penetrated" and that "new things can rush into [his] plenum displacing old things, things that were previously there" (45).

H119.10, B88.6   Jesús Arrabal   "Arrabal" denotes a region on the outskirts of a city. In the United States, we would understand this to be a reference to the suburbs, but in Mexico, Arrabal's home, the word indicates that part of the city occupied by the latest arrivals from the countryside—the poorest and most-neglected inhabitants of the urban sprawl. Jesús, therefore, stands for the idea of redemption for the preterite poor, those who live on the margins of capitalism.

H119.16, B88.12 "CIA" The comic reversal of expectation achieved here is reminiscent of Metzger's protest to Fallopian about the Peter Pinguid Society: "You're so right-wing you're left-wing" (H88.34). It serves as a reminder, too, of the fact that manifestations of the Tristero occur in contexts that sometimes shed positive, sometimes negative light on that organization, creating an impression that is by no means unambiguous.

H119.18, B88.14 Conjuración de los Insurgentes Anarquistas Conspiracy of the anarchist rebels.

H119.19, B88.15 the Flores Magón brothers Enrique, Ricardo and Jesús Flores Magón, jailed by the Mexican authorities at the turn of the century for publishing antigovernment propaganda, fled to the United States after their release, where they continued to publish the newspaper *La Regeneración*, the "anarcho-syndicalist" publication that Oedipa notices in Arrabal's greasy spoon (H121.5n).

H119.20, B88.16 Zapata Emiliano Zapata (1883–1919), a thorn in the side of successive revolutionary governments. He headed a peasant army ostensibly dedicated to the swifter accomplishment of land reform.

H119.22, B88.18 a yucateco A native of the Yucatán, and thus, like so many native peoples, representative of those displaced by the politics of majority rule.

H119.23, B88.19 *Their* Revolution. Presumably the anarchist revolution for which Jesús still waits.

H120.7, B88.35 "another world's intrusion" Politics and thermodynamics come together in Jesús's theory of miracles. The intrusion from outside of some form of knowledge—elsewhere referred to as revelation, the Word—constitutes the necessary infusion of new energy into a potentially closed system. In this sense, at least, the Tristero can be regarded as "miraculous," insofar as it intrudes into Oedipa's solipsistic existence.

Tanner points out that "the 'anarchist miracle' would not involve the intrusion of the 'sacred' world into our profane one; rather it would be a kind of 'revolution' leading to a whole new way of living together in this world. It would be 'another world'— but still secular. A mundane miracle" ("Crying" 187).

H120.16, B89.3 "He is too exactly and without flaw the thing we fight." "That this moral judgment is made by a champion of the poor named 'Jesus' is enough to suggest that Pierce represents a Satanic archetype, but the religious tensions here are more characteristically Pynchonian than those in the basic Christian antithesis. Pynchon's sympathy for anarchists such as Arrabal is based partly on their feeling for the preterite and partly on their championing of an absolute freedom that is the very antithesis of gnostic restraint—and that involves a dream of natural beneficence which anticipates the naturalistic norm toward which he is working" (Eddins 101).

H120.28, B89.13 without the miracle of Pierce to reassure him Pierce, Oedipa speculates, is the external energy source that sustains Jesús in his exiled opposition to the majority politics of his homeland. Without the provocation of this representative of all that he despises, Jesús, like so many others, might have run out of revolutionary steam and allowed himself to be assimilated into the undifferentiated mass of the Mexican people. The lesson is a pertinent one for Oedipa, who needs the Tristero as Jesús needs Pierce.

H120.30, B89.15 the majority priistas Members of the Institutional Revolution Party (PRI) that was for so long the completely dominant voice in postrevolutionary Mexican politics.

H121.1, B89.17 linking feature in a coincidence Oedipa here articulates what will later become a matter of great concern to her, the possibility that Pierce's presence at the center of all the manifestations of the Tristero may mean she is the victim of some elaborate plot.

H121.5, B89.21 the anarcho-syndicalist paper Published in Mexico, then in San Antonio and St. Louis by the Flores Magón brothers (H120.9n).

H121.11, B89.27 **"Has it really taken sixty years?"** If Jesús is being exact in his arithmetic, this would indicate that the action of the novel takes place in 1964.

H121.15, B89.30 **the city beach** At the far west end of Golden Gate Park, the city beach has long been a hangout for the homeless and the footloose of the city.

H121.26, B90.1 **DEATH** This ominous acronym comes as no surprise to the reader, who is by now well acquainted with the more threatening aspects of the Tristero. Eddins's reading, which invokes the later revelation that W.A.S.T.E. stands for "We Await Silent Tristero's Empire" (H169.1n), suggests that we are being exposed to the dark side of the "gnostic opposition" that informs his approach to Pynchon's work as a whole. "One of the definitive characteristics of gnostic empire, according to Voegelin, is its self-proclaimed immunity to criticism or questioning of any sort. Peremptory dealings with those who would open the System by calling its rationalizing gnosis into question are the stratagem by which the System seeks to remain closed, and thus impermeable" (96).

H122.7, B90.13 **Was The Horn so dedicated?** The question requires a bit of a double take on the reader's part, asking the reader to loop back to the "whiteness" to which everything in the laundromat is "dedicated," and hence to the irony of the laundromat's being situated in a "Negro neighborhood." Oedipa is essentially wondering if the Tristero is a racist organization. Once again a darker side of the Tristero is admitted as a possibility.

H122.10, B90.16 **songs in the lower stretches** Another indicator of Oedipa's increasing sense of connectedness with the preterite, or passed over, elements of her culture (See also H15.15n).

H122.29, B90.33 **ACDC** The acronym's more recognizable use as a colloquial expression for sexual ambivalence serves to reinforce the ambiguity that surrounds the Tristero.

H123.6, B91.2 **He was kissing his mother passionately** "Pynchon effectively mocks his own oedipal . . . motivation, as neurotic fictional creator, with the figure of the little [sic] boy who, kissing his mother goodbye (his using his tongue emphasizes the incestuous overtones), assures her repeatedly, 'I'll write, ma' " (Hall 67).

H123.28, B91.22 another voyeur This suggestion that Oedipa thinks of herself as a voyeur reminds us that she is still very much on the outside in relation to the alienated figures who appear to her throughout the night. Even the sympathy that leads her to embrace the alcoholic sailor does not initiate her into the ranks of the dispossessed, and she remains at a distance from those who appear to be linked loosely together by the symbolic horn. The last word we hear on the matter in fact indicates a kind of fear at the thought that she might "be hounded someday as far as joining Tristero itself" (H181.11). At the same time, the narrator's characterizing Oedipa as a voyeur conveys a sense of her embarrassment at this distancing apprehensiveness.

H123.32, B91.26 She grew so to expect it See H117.21n.

H124.8, B91.33 like the private eye Tanner is among the many critics who have associated the novel with the work of writers such as Chandler and MacDonald. He notes, however, that "it works in a reverse direction," moving from "a state of degree-zero mystery" to "a condition of increasing mystery and dubiety" (*Thomas Pynchon* 56).

Note that the effect of Oedipa's positioning of herself as the private eye—the good guy—very firmly places the Tristero (or whoever "They" may be) in the role of villain. Picking up on the "long-ago radio drama," Watson pursues a line of reasoning that ties Oedipa to this darker aspect: "Pierce Inverarity last spoke to her in the voice of just such a private eye, 'the Shadow'; and the book persistently identifies shadows with the Tristero. In becoming the detective, she becomes a part of the sinister force the detective is pursuing" (60).

H124.13, B91.38 this malignant, deliberate replication See H117.1n.

H124.17, B92.1 immobilizing her The effect of the proliferation of signs is paradoxical in relation to the novel as a whole, which, in its employment of metaphors associated with thermodynamics, appears to endorse the Tristero as a source of energy that runs counter to the culture's tendency toward stagnation and stasis. Schaub, in his response to Mendelson's somewhat positive reading of the "invigorating" increase in information (128), asserts what he calls "the ominous, paralytic aspect of this information increase" ("Open Letter" 95).

H124.25, B92.10 God knew how many citizens See Marcuse's description (H124.27n) for a picture of who these "citizens" might be. See also Michael Harrington's description in *The Other America: Poverty in the United States:* "The other America, the America of poverty, is hidden today in a way it never was before. Its millions are socially invisible to the rest of us. . . . Poverty is often off the beaten track. It always has been. The ordinary tourist never left the main highway and today he rides interstate turnpikes. . . . They [the poor] have no face, they have no voice. . . . They are dispossessed in terms of what the rest of the nation enjoyed, in terms of what the society could provide if it had the will. They live on the fringes, the margin. They watch the movies and read the magazines of affluent America and these tell them that they are internal exiles" (quoted in Petillon 167n).

Davidson sees Oedipa's glimpse of this segment of the population as part of the learning experience she undergoes throughout the novel. "Oedipa . . . knowing both worlds, can mediate between them. As she descends from the restrictive and constraining tower into the competitive, callous world of tycoon and entrepreneur, and then into the still-lower world of misfits and outcasts, she advantageously experiences the different levels of her society and gains something from each" (46).

H124.27, B92.11 not an act of treason Herbert Marcuse, in his conclusion to *One Dimensional Man,* suggests how we might nevertheless regard the actions of these outcasts as "revolutionary": "Underneath the conservative popular base is the substratum of outcasts and outsiders, the exploited and persecuted of other races and other colors, the unemployed and the unemployable. They exist outside the democratic process; their life is the most immediate and most real need for ending intolerable conditions and institutions. Thus their opposition is revolutionary even if their consciousness is not. Their opposition hits the system from with-out and is therefore not deflected by the system, it is an elementary force which violates the rules of the game, and in doing so, reveals it as a rigged game. The fact that they start refusing to play the game may be the fact which marks the beginning of the end of a period" (quoted in Dugdale 149).

H125.1, B92.18 could they? Perhaps a rather gratuitous, "Twilight Zone" kind of aside, but it does reflect Oedipa's unnerved state of mind.

H125.4, B92.22 jitney A jitney is in fact a small bus, though from the context one might be forgiven for thinking that Pynchon is referring to a taxi.

H125.21, B92.37 "My wife's in Fresno" "[Walter] Benjamin asserts that one of the archaic representatives of the storyteller is 'the trading seaman' the carrier of 'the lore of faraway places.' Odysseus of course fills this role in the *Odyssey*, but by the time Western culture has reached Pynchon's vision of San Francisco in *TCL49*, Odysseus has become the decrepit sailor Oedipa encounters on the rooming-house steps, a seaman who will never make it home to his wife in Fresno and who asks Oedipa to post 'a letter that looked like he'd been carrying it around for years'" (Duyfhuizen 86).

H125.31, B93.6 "Under the freeway." "Here is a 'monumental' metaphor: the WASTE system runs underneath the California free-way system and undermines it" (Couturier 12).

H125.33, B93.8 Cammed each night The sailor's dreams lift him temporarily out of the groove of the city's conventional day-to-day existence, the "furrow" that the virtuous and upright citizens of the republic dutifully plow.

H126.12, B93.19 like the memory bank to a computer of the lost A fine example of Pynchon's ability to use the language of technology in the service of a mournful lyricism. The mattress-as-memory links this moment and subsequent repetitions (H128.9n) with the Maxwell's Demon exchange in Nefastis's apartment (see H105–7).

H126.17, B93.24 actually held him Critics agree for the most part that this scene depicts Oedipa's intuitive recognition of her re-lationship with the outcasts of her society. For Mendelson, "her embrace of the old sailor is a tangible manifestation of the unlikely relations for which the Tristero is an emblem. Through the Tristero, Oedipa has learned to comfort the book's equivalent of that helpless figure to whom all successful quest-heroes must give succour" (141). Kolodny and Peters maintain that the embrace "is a recognition on her part of the value of the possibilities that might be contained in his warped visions of the world; it is a recognition, simultaneously, of all the possibilities of experience which are lost to us because our language has lost its multiplicity of reference, its suggestiveness" (82–83). For many, the scene is a pietà—Oedipa as Mary, mourning the death of possibility. In noting this, Petillon points to a parallel with Kerouac: "Kerouac's 'beat time' in San Francisco, where he walks around picking up butts from the street and, with Marylou, visits 'some drunken seaman in a flophouse on Mission Street,' more than foreshadows Oedipa's experience in the Embarcadero when, like a mourning Pietà, she nurses a dying sailor" (130).

Merrill, however, maintains that "Pynchon would not have us believe that we can transcend our suburban landscapes simply by embracing the downtrodden as so many spiritual brothers" (63), and he reminds us that Oedipa will very soon wish that the whole matter of the Trystero could be dismissed as a fantasy (H132.14).

H127.1, B93.39   She didn't know.   Oedipa never will quite know "Where else" the preterite might find a home, a resting place, other than in the darker corners and alleyways of our culture. She wonders to the very end whether she might not indeed have discovered "a real alternative to the exitlessness" of contemporary experience (H170.25), but she is never sure. The connection that she forges with the old sailor, and hence with all whom he represents, is ephemeral, loosening irrecoverably at precisely the time when she reverts to her mainline expectations, dreaming about rescuing the sailor by dressing him in a suit and giving him a bus ticket. "She reacts with the strategies of a person still possessed of a loving husband, a sane analyst, and an unbroken faith in the social system" (Watson 63).

H127.15, B94.12   A picture of a saint   What are we to make of the fact that the picture depicts Saint Narcissus (San Narciso), bishop of Jerusalem, performing a transformative miracle? The image invokes contradictory impressions, pointing at one and the same time to the narcissism that is clearly responsible for much that is negative about contemporary American culture, and to the idea of the miraculous that informs the novel's more optimistic side.

We have already noted Palmeri's claim that the miracles of Saint Narcissus are invoked as a counter to the sterility of the self-love depicted in the Ovidian account of Narcissus (H65.21n). As Palmeri points out, however, the bishop's miracles were appropriated by the church, via Eusebius's official history, thus "routinizing" their charismatic character in the name of institutional necessity. The picture may thus suggest that our culture can appropriate even the dreams in which the preterite experience freedom from the furrow of the quotidian.

H128.9, B94.39 Register A A register, in computer terms, is a physical memory device of a capacity measured in bits. The mattress is conceived as such a memory storage system, and the knowledge encoded in it is measurable.

H128.18, B95.8 massive destructions of information The comparison of the mattress to a computer memory, coupled with this reference to information loss, takes us back to Oedipa's efforts to understand Nefastis's machine, and reinforces the notion that Nefastis may be familiar with early speculations about the relationship between entropy and the surrender of knowledge that occurs when a computer's memory is reset. The burning of the mattress, of course, scarcely represents the resetting of a memory device, since the device itself goes up in smoke, but it does once again associate an increase in uncertainty with entropy gain. In comparison with the memories chemically encoded into the mattress, the thermal energy of the blaze is disordered, randomly distributed, highly entropic.

Couturier finds the comparison invidious, charging that "[Oedipa's] reaction is again that of the materialist: a man, like a mattress, is no more than a text crammed with information. When the text is burnt, there is nothing left" (16). Hayles, however, finds room for a more spiritually oriented reading: "The destruction of information in the sailor's mattress signifies what is lost when the human spirit is extinguished. The total of mass and energy may remain constant, but the delicate webs that connect neurons to thoughts, electrons to memory and feeling, are gone forever" (115).

According to Tanner, "this sense of whole constructed mental worlds of dream and memory—she groups those of the saint, the clairvoyant, the paranoid, and she could have added the artist—vanishing irreversibly away . . . is another linking of rubbish and fantasies suggested by the sign W.A.S.T.E. Do we live in fantasy because things have usurped too much of the human domain; or is the visible accumulation of junk around us only the result of our proclivity for fantasy-life?" ("V." 45).

H128.25, B95.15 the irreversible process It is not clear what Oedipa is thinking of in specifying a *particular* process here. Irreversibility and irreversible processes are terms drawn from the physical sciences having a general relevance to all physical events: "A birch log, for example, cannot be burnt twice. One cannot take the hot flue gases of a wood fire and the warmth of the fire and from these reconstitute an unburnt log, fresh air, and room chilliness. Passage from the burnt state—the hot flue gases and a warm room—to the pre-burnt state—a birch log, fresh air, and a cold room—is impossible, or at most, highly improbable" (H. A. Bent, quoted in Bolton 194). The ashes and heat of the burnt mattress cannot be reconstituted into the set of memories that represent the living human beings who have slept in that flophouse on that bed. Ultimately, Oedipa's recognition is of the inevitability of death, the inexorable march of time in one direction only.

H128.30, B95.19 Behind the initials was a metaphor Pynchon here relies heavily on etymological associations to achieve his purpose. Cowart notes that "*delirare*, the Latin word meaning 'to be crazy,' actually means being out (*de*) of the furrow (*lira*). Just as we say someone is 'unhinged'—using a metaphor that is becoming increasingly unconscious—the Romans said that one was 'unfurrowed'" (*Art of Allusion* 108). Recall that the sailor is said to be "cammed each night out of that safe furrow" that represents the so-called sane world of day-to-day activities, and note that Oedipa finds herself very shortly "trembling, unfurrowed" as her mind makes an unaccustomed leap across time (H129.9).

H128.31, B95.21   The saint . . . protect us from.   In this list of emblematic figures, all of them uniquely connected with the world they inhabit, the clairvoyant stands out in interesting contrast to the epileptic of an earlier passage (H95.5n), whose "lapse in recall" renders inaccessible whatever insight may have been gained during the fit. The clairvoyant's trance, characterized by a similar lapse, nonetheless supposedly yields knowledge from some spiritual plane outside the reach of ordinary means of apprehension.

The mention of the dreamer inevitably suggests a Freudian dimension to this whole passage, a fact that does not escape Palmeri. "Freud's method for converting oppositions to complementarities in analyzing the language of dreams provides Pynchon with a prototype of language that would not be bound by the law of excluded middles. Lacking the negative, dream words and images produce antithetical meanings like those of key words in ancient languages: for example, the Latin *altus* ('high' and 'deep') and *sacer* ('holy' and 'polluted'), and the Greek *pharmakon/-os* ('poison' and 'antidote,' 'scapegoat' and 'king'). In a crucial passage, Oedipa recognizes that the dreamer, the saint, and the paranoid exist in a special relation to language because '[their] puns probe ancient fetid shafts and tunnels of truth' " (988).

Berressem regards these figures as representative of those who have "transcended the realm and laws of discourse. They are outside language and the metaphorical construction of reality" (107).

H129.4, B95.26   the same special relevance to the word   "Word" here points to language in general, rather than to the concept of revealed truth, as it does elsewhere. Thus the saint, the clairvoyant, the paranoid, and the dreamer are said to "act in special relevance to" language, a claim that is not immediately clear in its implications. Although Pynchon is not notable for his carelessness of expression, it may be that Palmeri's paraphrase, "exist in a special relation to language," conveys the intent of the sentence more clearly.

Tanner notes that Oedipa's list could have included the artist ("V." 45), a suggestion that derives some authority from the musings of Fausto Maijstral in V. "Living as he does much of the time in a world of metaphor, the poet is always acutely conscious that metaphor has no value apart from its function; that it is a device, an artifice. So that while others may look on the laws of physics as legislation, and God as a human form with beard measured in lightyears and nebulae for sandals, Fausto's kind are alone with the task of living in a universe of things which simply are, and cloaking that mindlessness with comfortable and pious metaphor" (V. 322). The "mindlessness" that Fausto refers to may be "whatever it is the word is there, buffering, to protect us from."

H129.6, B95.28 The act of metaphor Hayles points to the difficulties caused by the syntax of this passage, which links "inside" to metaphor as "truth" and "outside" to metaphor as "lie." If the associations were reversed, Hayles argues, the passage "one of the text's most enigmatic" would be easier to understand, since the "safe" insider might be inclined to dismiss the threatening, disruptive implications of metaphor by branding them as misleading, while the "lost" outsider might more willingly accept the challenge, and hence the possibility, that metaphors might represent (115–16). Palmeri appears to have read the passage in something like this reversed sense: "If we take Tristero as a pointer to various species of loss, from psychological abandonment to physical death, then being outside, lost, at least enables one to make an attempt at telling the truth, whereas the safety of the inside produces lies, approved genres, and the authorized mail system" (993).

Attempting a "syntactically stronger reading," Hayles suggests that, for "those inside, metaphors may be a thrust at truth because they hint at the constructed nature of reality; for those outside, they are a lie because like any other language, they cannot penetrate the construction to touch reality as such" (116). This is similar to Schaub's view: "From the outside, metaphor is only a 'buffer,' while from the 'inside, safe,' metaphor provides access to that very realization, and is therefore a 'thrust at the [sic] truth'" (38). The link with Fausto's attitude toward metaphor is clear and, retrospectively, helps us see how far "outside" the detached poet has become by the time he writes his journal. Oedipa, uncertain of where she stands, perceives both aspects of metaphorical language.

For Mendelson, being "inside" means being "joined to the world in which moral and metaphoric connections, links of responsibility across time and among persons, endorsed by a hieratic vision, actually exist" (42). The outsider, in contrast, can see only arbitrariness in the connections posited by metaphor, lies designed to assert unity where there is only incoherence. Mendelson, as do many other critics, stresses the importance of the fact that metaphor is here seen in a dual light, both as an attempt to tell the truth *and* as a lie. "Things exist in the polymorphous realm of both/and, rather than either/or" (Coates 126), a realm that distinctly resembles the world of *The Courier's Tragedy* in the fourth act, when a "new mode of expression" is said to have taken over, a mode that is neither literal nor metaphoric, but clearly takes up an unsettling position in between.

The language of the novel as a whole mirrors this approach to metaphor, as we follow Oedipa through the twists and turns of her quest. Just as she is unsure whether the "metaphor of God knew how many parts" with which she is faced points unequivocally either to a real Tristero or to a hoax, we are never certain whether the language we are reading corresponds to some ascertainable reality outside the text or simply points up the arbitrariness of the relationship between language and meaning.

Readers interested in a Lacanian reading of this passage are referred to Berressem (107–8).

H129.9, B95.31 Trembling, unfurrowed In the transition from the plowed furrow to the phonograph groove, Hayles sees a movement from the agricultural to the technological (119).

H129.23, B96.5 high magic to low puns The poignant fact remains, however, that high magic cannot preserve the insights that are granted those who act in a special relation to language. The truth of those insights may be like the truth that Nefastis maintains is present in the congruity of the two entropy equations—a private, more or less inaccessible truth that can be sensed from the outside only by inference. Nothing Oedipa knows is capable of preserving either the sailor or his visions.

H129.25, B96.7 music made purely of Antarctic loneliness An invocation, surely, of that other ancient mariner whose compelling "music" makes of the Wedding Guest "A sadder and a wiser man." Eddins links the sailor's vision with the experiences of Hugh Godolphin in *V.:* "In the polar wasteland of his delirium tremens, the old drunk has had a vision of the ultimate alienation, of the static and dehumanized Kingdom of Death" (96). Like the sailor's, Godolphin's horrifying insight cannot survive its passage into the public world.

H129.27, B96.9 She gave him goodbye A (presumably) deliberately archaic locution, intended to capture the solemnity of Oedipa's experience with the old sailor. She blesses him in leaving, knowing that this is all she can do for him.

H130.3, B96.17 She had to look closely Dugdale uses this as an example of the novel's manipulation of point of view. Noting that the "unvarying gray sickness" that so distressed Mucho when he worked at the car lot is in fact composed of "a pile of dissociated objects, randomly thrown together," he points out that " 'WASTE' proves to be 'W.A.S.T.E.' when Oedipa gets near enough to the inscription to see the periods that separate the letters and thereby hint at a wholly different subsurface meaning. Like the letters, the groups that patronize the Tristero are discrete and distinguishable, often unaware of one another's existence. And yet, from another point of view, the periods vanish and the groups merge into a continuity of human 'waste' or preterition" (133).

For Kolodny and Peters, the moment of discovery is a positive one, leading as it does to Oedipa's active participation in the Tristero via the W.A.S.T.E. system. "If previously she had only sought out the Tristero, *now* she has actively participated in it. And, in so doing, Oedipa has at once embraced the dreams, hallucinations, and sufferings of another human being and simultaneously committed herself to the possibilities of other realities and to the viability of other modes of consciousness" (84).

H130.16, B96.30 infected by its gray The Civic Center, the representative of mainstream culture, appears to emanate a kind of gray sickness.

H130.24, B96.37   The landscape lost all variety.   The reader is presumably sensitized by now to this sort of indication of stagnation through references to lack of differentiation.

H131.4, B97.8   She was back where she'd started   The circular nature of the night's activities suggests a kind of exitlessness that runs counter to some of the associations that build up around the Tristero. At the same time, of course, given the possibility—still alive at the end of the novel—that Oedipa will remain trapped in a private, paranoid universe of her own fabrication, this circularity is strangely apposite.

H131.22, B97.26   There would have to be collisions.   Oedipa still clings to her old order ways of thinking about the world. Her vision of the way things are does not admit of the possibility that other orders of being might exist, in which—as in fact turns out to be the case—collisions would not "have" to happen. She "finds in this silent ballroom full of dancing couples a cultural formation to which she is alien—a system of communal order inside a seeming anarchy that occurs beyond her particular patterns of logic" (Duyfhuizen 80).

H131.24, B97.27   some unthinkable order of music   Reminiscent perhaps of the somewhat more comically conceived performances of the Duke di Angelis quartet in "Entropy," which consist of all the members of the group thinking their way through a song rather than actually playing it out loud.

H132.2, B97.36   only demoralized   If we recall that Oedipa seems ready to think of language as a "buffer," protecting us from the harshness of reality, we can readily see that her having "no name" for this experience would be demoralizing. The unnerving silence of the deaf-mute dance points to a reality unmediated by language, something quite outside the experience of our college-educated middle-class housewife.

H132.14, B98.7   she wanted it all to be fantasy   The responsibility implicit in the complex order suggested by the proliferating symbols is more than Oedipa wishes to take on. If it were all fantasy, she could dismiss it, shrug it off, and return to the relative comfort of her tower in Kinneret. If it is real, she must face the burden that she momentarily assumed when she embraced the old sailor.

H133.12, B98.37 A Gewehr 43 A gas-operated semi-automatic rifle developed by the Germans during World War II.

H134.11, B99.26 "Speer and his ministry of cretins" Albert Speer was the Nazi minister of armaments and munitions during World War II. Although all accounts credit Speer with bringing about increased efficiency in industrial production, Hilarius is clearly blaming him for the malfunction of his rifle.

H134.28, B100.1 that cantankerous Jew Freud.

H135.4, B100.9 Biedermeyer furniture Furniture, that is, which represents comfortable middle-class values. The name comes from "Papa Biedermeier," a caricatured bourgeois character whose exploits were chronicled in a series of popular poems published in Germany in the early nineteenth century. The name was passed on to a style of furniture that flourished from 1815–1848.

H135.16, B100.21 "They replicate" Schaub sees this as a recapitulation of the "malignant, deliberate replication" (H124.13) of the post horn symbol that Oedipa encounters during her nighttime journey through San Francisco ("Open Letter" 93).

H135.31, B100.36 "His name was Zvi." A variant of the Hebrew name Zevi, which can mean "deer" or "wolf."

H136.15, B101.13 the distinction begins to vanish We will see the evidence of this in Mucho's LSD-induced "vision of consensus" (H143.5).

H136.17, B101.15 relative paranoia Hilarius, who appears to have completely abandoned his wits, rather paradoxically claims a state of mind that, in terms of the extremes articulated by the novel, represents a relatively sane middle ground. Possessed neither by a vision of total paranoia, in which the self would be seen as powerless, nor by one of a total absence of order, Hilarius maintains a healthy distinction between himself and the world outside himself, avoiding both Mucho's utter surrender of self and Driblette's "megalomaniac doom" (Eddins 104).

H136.33, B101.29 "Buchenwald" German concentration camp built near Weimar in 1937 and operated until 1945. The site of medical experimentation on live human subjects.

H137.15, B102.5 "Eichmann" Adolf Eichmann (1906–62). Head of Section IV B4 in the Reich Central Security Office during World War II. Eichmann's office was responsible for tracking down Jews and incarcerating them in concentration camps. He escaped after the war and was captured in Buenos Aires by Israeli agents in 1961. He was hanged in 1962.

H137.20, B102.11 Brechtian vignettes Performances in the manner of Bertoldt Brecht (1898–1956). The logic of this is a little hard to follow. Perhaps the solemness and unrelenting didacticism of Brecht's epic theater is being gently mocked here. Being woken up in the middle of the night to watch excerpts from Brecht's plays may be enough to constitute mental torture. Possibly there is some loose allusion to the "alienation effect" with which Brecht sought to keep audiences off balance, aware that they were watching a performance. There is some irony to be found in the fact that Brecht was a Marxist.

H137.31, B102.20 "If I'd been a real Nazi" Most obviously, Hilarius appeals to Oedipa's knowledge of Nazi antisemitism. Freud was Jewish, making Jung a likelier model for the Nazi Hilarius to emulate. Also, one might suppose that Jung's concept of mythic archetypes as the foundation of human personality would be appealing to the Nazi sensibility.

H138.2, B102.25 "solfeggio" A voice exercise based on the sol-fa syllables.

H138.21, B103.5 "Cherish it!" According to Eddins, this is "a warning to preserve her private sense of the transcendental from the mania for a monistic materialism" (103). Johnston claims that, "in valorizing fantasy as the essential component of individual identity, Hilarius assumes a world in which normative behavior is no longer possible or desirable" (65). Given Oedipa's sense of loss at her inability to preserve the visions of the drunken sailor, we can assume that Hilarius's advice will strike a chord.

H139.20, B103.35 "Edna Mosh" Colville offers an interesting, if somewhat disturbing, speculation based on this exchange: "If you have to say Edna Mosh into the speaker to have it come out as

Oedipa Maas, then a whole code may be involved which would displace the sound and meaning of *The Crying of Lot 49* in its entirety" (26). While this seems somewhat extreme, the novel's concern with issues of communication certainly lends some importance to Mucho's claim, which points to the inevitable distortion that occurs in any communication channel. As many critics have noted, Oedipa becomes a receiver, attempting to resolve the signals that emanate from her world into a discrete and organized message which will contain a meaning equivalent to the meaning of that world. Signals, however, are subject to interference, in the form of "noise," which reduces the probability that any given signal will be received in precisely the form in which it was transmitted. The ambiguity that Oedipa senses in her attempts to decode the Tristero is the novel's equivalent of noise. She has no way of knowing how closely the messages she is receiving resemble the messages that have been "sent."

H139.33, B104.8 "If there aren't any"   Oedipa seems to sense in Hilarius's situation an analogy to her own. If there are in reality no agents of the Tristero, then Oedipa will be forced to conclude that she is crazy.

H140.22, B!04.30 "He's losing his identity"   "This hallucinogenic evasion, which is much like Hilarius's own misguided attempt to sanitize the dark corners of the unconscious through Freudian psychology, is Mucho's chosen form of coping with—i.e., denying— the complex directness of things" (Eddins 104). Eddins also reads Mucho's disintegration as part of the novel's "parody of Pentecost," arguing that, although Mucho "speaks in myriad tongues . . . this glossolalia culminates in a Babel of quasi-mystical nonsense, thus marking him as a gnostic apostle of entropy" (104).

H140.14, B104.22 "Ringo Starr . . . Righteous Brothers"   Ringo Starr, born Richard Starkey, was the drummer for the Beatles. Chubby Checker, born Ernest Evans, popularized the Twist. The Righteous Brothers, Bill Medley and Bobby Hatfield, were noted for their close harmony ballads. Insofar as name changes indicate a change in identity, the figures Oedipa chooses are perhaps not altogether randomly selected.

H141.25, B105.25 "His E string"   There appears to be something of a contradiction between the heightened perception that the drug affords Mucho and its overall effect on his personality. The kind of subtle discriminations that he is now capable of—here represented by the acuteness of his tonal sense—would seem to point toward just that degree of differentiation which the novel finds to be absent from the culture at large.

H141.33, B105.33 "He was real." Again, a positive insight afforded by the drug. Mucho is speculating whether it might not be possible to rescue the studio musician from the blandness implicit in the music he is playing, to restore him, ironically enough, to full, unique individuality. Of course, he immediately goes on to point out that it would be possible to dispense with live musicians altogether.

H142.16, B106.10 "Rich, chocolaty, goodness" "The Logos is caricatured here as a mindless aural wallowing that signposts only chaos. The disguising of this chaos as spiritual unity returns us to the elemental irony of gnostic pretensions" (Eddins 104).

"The ideas of homogenization and consumerism come together in Mucho's 'vision of consensus,' which is a *reductio ad absurdum* of the effects of the media on the USA, altering people 'till they all coincide'" (Dugdale 147).

According to Slade, "Mucho has become Echo" (169).

H144.22, B107.37 "N.A.D.A." "Nada," Spanish for nothing. Mucho's retreat into himself, which protects him from the effects of the void represented by the sign, is an avenue of escape that must seem attractive to Oedipa, who will come to confront a similar emptiness as her quest progresses (H171.13n).

"The word . . . should remind Pynchon's readers of the lady V., who takes pleasure in contemplating 'Nothing'" (Slade 168).

The sign also reminds us of Hemingway's "A Clean Well-Lighted Place" (among other stories), with its understated invocation of a profound hollowness at the center of human experience.

☞ Chapter 6

H147.6, B109.17 *Humbert Humbert cats* Humbert Humbert is the protagonist of Nabokov's novel *Lolita* and hence a prototype for the older man obsessed with very young girls. The jury is still out on the question of Pynchon's contact with Nabokov at Cornell University. For a long time it was asserted that Pynchon took a course from Nabokov, with the accompanying suggestion that he was somehow personally known to the great man. Hollander devotes some space to dismissing this possibility, having determined that Pynchon was not actually enrolled in Nabokov's class, which he may simply have audited (12).

H147.9, B110.3 *nymphet* Another reference to Lolita, who is Humbert Humbert's "nymphet."

H148.5, B110.29 **She should have felt more classically scorned** Although Oedipa's relationships with men seem doomed to failure, the novel maintains a certain cool distance from the issue of love. This line is typical of the way sexual and marital connectedness are downplayed in the novel by situating them within some kind of convention—here the "classical" paradigm of betrayal. Pierce is originally seen as the fairy-tale prince, while marriage to Mucho is therapy.

H148.16, B110.40 **a wife named Grace** Whose name Oedipa will appropriate temporarily, perhaps in an effort to find grace in the midst of the threatening, exhausting lead-up to the stamp auction at the end of the novel (H171.30).

H148.31, B111.15 **not a matter of Bortz's response** A somewhat enigmatic line, made more so by the vagueness of the referent for the word "it." The connection appears to be with the previous sentence's process of achieving a "studentlike" appearance. Is Oedipa thinking that she may be able to represent her interest in the Tristero in an "innocent" light by suggesting that it is purely academic in nature? Why would Grace's response ever be an issue, since she is not connected with Oedipa's quest except tangentially by marriage to Bortz?

H149.1, B111.18 a pile of charred rubble She is on her way to find out that Driblette is dead. The destruction of the bookstore assumes in retrospect an even more disquieting character.

H149.26, B112.2 "Winthrop Tremaine" "It is, of course, no accident that Winthrop Tremaine, the Swastika salesman, should have as his first name the last name of one of the oldest New England Mayflower families, the Winthrops. Pynchon seems to want to create a link between Nazism and the fanatic early American Puritan persecution of Quakers, witches, Indians, and other 'heretics' and consequently the very foundation of America, which seems to be an important background element in the novel's 'tapestry' " (Colville 27). Perhaps, too, Pynchon brings in the TV show "Johnny Tremaine" as a way of providing a further diminution of the American past.

H150.7, B112.16 This is America Schaub picks up on the use of the word "unfurl" and links this sentence with the tapestry motif begun by the Varo painting. "Here the painting, like the Narcissus myth, has been assumed into the fabric of the novel and is part of the social vision of a culture weaving itself in time, each generation responsible for the ongoing expansion. At the same time, there is no given pattern to follow" (34).

Oedipa here reveals overtly a sense of responsibility that perhaps accounts for her earlier need to hold the drunken sailor and for her instinctive understanding of the alienation represented by the people whom she observes during her long night in San Francisco. She will increasingly regard her quest as an inquiry into the nature of the republic as a whole, finally reaching the conclusion that the legacy that Pierce has left her is in some sense America itself (H178.14).

For Slade, Oedipa's self-castigation is evidence that Pynchon believes that "human choice [can] resist entropy or alter systems" (133).

H151.2, B113.3 "the historical Wharfinger" Nicholson sees the antihistorical response of the graduate student, and Bortz's acquiescence in it, as a continuation of Driblette's dismissal of the factual aspects of the play. "As the novel progresses, Oedipa begins to learn the limitations of her conventional critical devotion to the word, and seeks instead, from Bortz and other sources, the sort of wider historical understanding necessary to contextualise the significance of word and text" (92). The graduate student is, of course, articulating an orthodox New Critical position.

H151.23, B113.24 "K. da Chingado" Evidently Mexican Spanish would allow "chingado" to mean "fucked," in the sense of "in deep trouble." "K. da" reads as *"quedar,"* to remain, giving "permanently fucked" as a possible reading of the publisher's name.

H151.25, B113.26 "Offset." Bortz, whose interests place him closer to the beginning of printing than to its modern developments, may simply be expressing contempt for a new-fangled process, not more than twenty years old at this point. One can speculate, also, that pages printed using the offset process are more likely to smudge than those printed with the older letterpress process.

H151.27, B113.27 "Corrupt." Bortz has no patience with a text that does not conform to his idea of the "correct" version of the play. Oedipa can no longer afford the luxury of this bibliographic fastidiousness, since she has come to view the experience of the Tristero quest as a text (a metaphor of God knew how many parts) with many possible variants.

H152.6, B113.38 "hardly any responsibility toward the word" A reminder that Driblette's position with regard to Wharfinger's play was diametrically opposed to Bortz's. Unlike the academic, with his concern for the purity of the printed text, Driblette was content to work from smudged mimeographs, concerned with capturing the "spirit" of the playwright's vision. Both Mendelson (125) and Eddins (99) note that Driblette's approach implies a radical solipsism that leaves the individual bereft of any recourse to an ordering principle existing independently of the self. Bortz's position, one might argue, leaves him similarly isolated, in that it seeks to dismiss as "corrupt" any version of the Word that does not conform to a preconceived pattern.

H152.20, B114.9 "Randy walked into the Pacific" The suggestion is strongly made that Driblette commits suicide, "the logical culmination of an exclusive devotion to the spirit" (Mendelson 125).

Oedipa's inquiries, however, immediately lead to a reminder of the Tristero's violence toward those who cross its purposes. Driblette's decision to name the unnameable in the production that Oedipa sees may well be connected in sinister fashion to his death.

H152.29, B114.17   now she kept a silence   "She behaves, in other words, precisely as do those who obey the Tristero acronym W.A.S.T.E., We Await Silent Tristero's Empire" (Watson 65). Oedipa is growing increasingly afraid of what she may discover.

H152.31, B114.19   They are stripping from me   Couturier notes that this is the only time Oedipa's thoughts are presented by an omniscient narrator, arguing that this may indicate a loss of control on her part over "the narrative itself" (27).

For Watson, the stripping away represents Oedipa's increasing involvement with the Tristero: "She is becoming, in other words, a de facto member of the Inamorati Anonymous, a typically subvocal and secretive offshoot of the Tristero consisting of people who have despairingly sworn off love" (62). The involuntary nature of the process that leads to Oedipa's isolation may run counter to this assertion, however.

Langland regards the departure of these men from Oedipa's life in a positive light, inasmuch as it frees her to rely on herself and to shed the social assumptions that have controlled her in the past (205).

The "fluttering curtain" reminds Schaub of the tapestry in the Varo painting (34).

We ought, too, to remember the two other explicit references to the stripping away of layers—first in the Strip Botticelli game with Metzger (H41.10) and most enigmatically in Oedipa's flight of fancy about the Tristero as striptease dancer (H54.14n).

H153.3, B114.23   gropes like a child   Mucho's retreat inward is the novel's most explicit image of the solipsism that threatens the individual in contemporary America. The references to childhood link his choice to that of Metzger, the child actor who does not want to grow up.

H153.6, B114.26   what has passed . . . for love   Oedipa's choice of words is revealing, indicating her erstwhile willingness to settle for a relationship based on emotions that only "pass" for love.

H154.20, B115.31 "You think a man's mind is a pool table?" Oedipa has been placed in a difficult situation here. Her initial speculation, that Driblette may have been acting on "some whim" when he included the line naming the Tristero, is met with the opinion that this is unlikely, that Driblette was probably giving expression to some inner turmoil. However, when she seizes on this and expands it to infer a drastic change in Driblette's life, Bortz immediately derides her mechanistic, cause-and-effect assumptions. His reference is to the often-used illustration of Newtonian laws of motion, the billiard table, on which (in principle) the movement of the balls can be charted independently of the direction of time. Oedipa is grasping at straws and seems momentarily to have forgotten her vision of the irreversible process.

Implicit in these exchanges is the novel's constant negotiation of the middle ground that links two extremes. Here Oedipa swings from a version of mere chance—a whim—to a thoroughly deterministic explanation, only to find no solid footing in either direction. The reference to the pool table situates us in the realm of physical processes, where one of the most notorious attempts to reconcile contradictory opposites is to be found in the principle of complementarity, which seeks to accommodate the wave/particle duality of light. The effect is that we are forced to confront a way of knowing that refuses identification with either of two familiar possibilities—just as, in the play, Oedipa notes the intrusion of a new mode of expression, something between the literal and the metaphorical, "a new and problematical area of semantic dubiety," in Tanner's terms (*Thomas Pynchon* 59).

H155.12, B116.14 "Scurvhamites" Newman likens the "gaudy clockwork of the doomed" that is run by the Scurvhamites' "opposite Principle" to "the Calvinist approach to enterprise," which has led to "an industrial society fallen into inertia and homogeneity" (75).

Eddins finds a parallel between the "brute automatism" of the Scurvhamite vision and the "all too pervading completeness" of the order imposed on the universe by the "demiurge" of early gnosticism (92).

There seems little doubt that this passage can be read, in Hayles's terms, as a "parable of co-optation" (119), emblematic of the way in which contemporary society has been able to absorb even the most disruptive of counterculture impulses and appropriate them to its own ends. The "most pure" origins of the great American experiment are invoked ironically here.

H156.16, B117.10 "the brute Other" The Scurvhamite sense of the appropriateness of the Tristero as a symbol for the soulless "Other" is given some legitimacy by Oedipa's (and our own) sense of the darker aspects of the organization.

H156.20, B117.14 nothing more then to put it off with Oedipa is more and more possessed by a version of the "ritual reluctance" that characterizes the tone of the play after the middle of the fourth act.

H158.16, B118.34 "neither tempest nor strife" An interesting double perspective is achieved here. For the reader, the echo is of the familiar inscription on the New York City Post Office building, linking the Tristero couriers very much with the present and serving ironically to remind us of the Tristero's oppositional status, its tendency to disrupt and appropriate the functions of the "legitimate" lines of communication.

The inscription is itself an adaptation of a passage from Herodotus's *Histories* praising the dedication of the couriers of the Persian king Xerxes. The passage appears in Bartlett as follows: "Not snow, no, nor rain, nor heat, nor night keeps them from accomplishing their appointed courses with all speed." The Tristero couriers, therefore, are clearly educated men, ready with a classical allusion even under the stress of battle.

H158.25, B119.2 a few fragments A typical mingling of the real with the fabricated, with no way for the reader to distinguish between them. Motley's work contains hundreds of footnotes, most of them not in English. The task of determining which, if any, might be regarded as "ambiguous" in the appropriate way is monumental. Seed appears to have undertaken it nonetheless, since he claims quite unequivocally that "the footnote in Motley does not exist" (127). Dugdale notes that the reference to the pamphlet on anarchism may be specific, but that its real relevance lies in the link it forges with other references to anarchism in the novel (176).

H159.5, B119.14 In late December Although Pynchon mentions Motley's *Rise of the Dutch Republic,* he does not seem to be basing his account on that source. According to Motley, Orange "entered the capital in the afternoon of the 23rd of September" (420) and not in December, when he was in fact in Ghent (448). Also, Motley does not mention the "junta of Calvinist fanatics," noting only that the invitation to Orange came from the Estates-General itself, which "had unanimously united in a supplication that he would incontinently transport himself to the city of Brussels" (416). As Pynchon seems to have discovered, however, the Council, or "Committee" as he calls it, indeed "dictated all decisions of the Estates-General," including, presumably, the decision to invite Orange to the city. Cammaerts provides some confirmation when he claims that "since August 1577 Brussels had been practically in the hands of the Commune, represented by a Council of Eighteen" (192).

Whether the Council actually "threw out" Leonard I seems debatable, though Pynchon's account of the replacement of the Thurn and Taxis monopoly by a "loyal adherent of Orange" is evidently accurate. "When Leonard von Taxis, faithful to his oath, was continuing to serve the governorships of Don John of Austria and then of Alexander Farnese . . . the office of Postmaster General for Brussels was being taken over by the Orangist Jean Hinchaert, Lord of Ohain" (Delepinne 75, my translation).

H159.22, B119.30 Calavera Spanish for "skull." Another reminder of the potentially threatening nature of the Tristero.

H160.17, B120.16 His constant theme, disinheritance. The Tristero is seen to be the representative of those Americans who have been dispossessed of the legacy of the past.

H160.24, B120.23 the muted post horn The coiled horn had been part of the armorial bearings of the Thurn and Taxis family since the Emperor Maximilian had added it in the early sixteenth century (Harlow 62).

H161.12, B121.3 some version of herself Oedipa has transformed Driblette's original remark somewhat. He had suggested that a "part" of her might vanish, the part that is "so concerned, God knows how, with [the] little world" of the play (H79.33–H80.1).

Oedipa has expanded this into a whole "version" of herself, indicating, perhaps, the degree to which the search for the Tristero has possessed her—has become a journey of self-discovery.

H161.24, B121.15 a transient, winged shape Another of the novel's annunciatory images. The fragile remnant of Driblette's spirit may be what Oedipa needs to guide her toward some truth about the Tristero. It may be the revelation that will energize her once more.

H161.32, B121.21 the reason they got rid of Hilarius Oedipa appears to have no doubt that the Tristero is in some way behind the desertion of these other men.

H162.20, B122.3 But there was silence. The Paracletian implications of Oedipa's attempt at communication with Driblette are not brought to fruition. The silence that marks her inability to recover whatever truth Driblette may have possessed is as disturbing as the proliferation of signs that has so exhausted her during her journey through the nighttime city.

H163.13, B122.28 should Bortz have exfoliated The reader is being invited to judge the appropriateness of Bortz's speculations, the development of which seems to have become "a species of cute game" (H162.31). He takes the "mere words" of accounts such as Blobb's and elaborates them "lushly" into Hollywood-style scenarios, the "unnatural roses" of this passage. Such speculations, however, conceal the reality of the historical processes that take place in the secret darkness, under the rose. Pynchon is picking up on his own earlier story, "Under the Rose," which became the Egyptian chapter of *V.*, in which, beneath the surface of the tourists' Baedeker land, Armageddon is approached and avoided according to a complex dance of intrigue and compromise.

Hall (69) points out that Bortz's hypothesizing is in fact vindicated when we later learn of the schism that "split[s] the Tristero wide open" during the French Revolution (H172.18). Hall also notes that Bortz's speculations are the product of an "anti-scholastic, anti-empiricist method" that runs counter to his earlier endorsement of New Critical principles (H151.2n).

H163.23, B122.38 Private local posts "Between important towns rival messengers operated; in 1638 there were twelve competing for the business between Brussels and Antwerp" (Harlow 73). Harlow makes no mention of the closing of the Thurn and Taxis offices, recording only that the struggle for control of the mails in the region was waged for a hundred years or more.

H164.3, B123.10 Peace of Westphalia The conventional terminal point of the Thirty Years' War, which began in 1618 and ended with the signing of the treaty on October 24, 1648. The effect of the treaty was to strengthen the rule of the many princes of Europe over their individual principalities, and to weaken the already diminished power of the Holy Roman Emperor—hence the "descent into particularism."

H164.19, B123.24 I propose that we merge Despite the fact that this is a flight of fancy on Bortz's part, there is some suggestion here of the ambiguity of Tristero's ideological position—the possibility inherent in the W.A.S.T.E. acronym that one day the suppressed may assume imperial authority and become the suppressor. "Any prince tries to start his own courier system, we suppress it," Konrad suggests.

H165.20, B124.17 paranoia recedes Mendelson suggests that Pynchon tempts the reader here with a "safe" way to read the novel, analogous to the safe way the Thurn and Taxis monopolists come to view the "secular" Tristero. "The book offers the possibility that its religious metaphor is only a metaphor," Mendelson claims, "but if the book were founded on this limited possibility, the remaining portions of the book would make no sense, and there would be little reason to write it in the first place" (121).

Perhaps Bortz, in spinning this tale, is similarly attempting to seduce Oedipa into thinking of the Tristero in purely secular terms.

H165.27, B124.24 Proclamation of 9th Frimaire The *Bulletin des lois de la République Française* records only three laws issued on that date, none of them regulating the postal service in any way.

H166.16, B125.5 anxious that her revelation not expand Oedipa has progressed so far along the road to self-discovery that she is now reluctant to lose ground and be subsumed once more into an all-encompassing structure akin to the tower in the Varo painting.

H167.1, B125.20 Training rebels A reminder of the curious ambiguity that surrounds Fallopian's group, which is so right wing it is left wing, according to Metzger (H88.33). The Tristero presents a similarly fuzzy ideological profile.

H167.29, B126.7 It had occurred to her. Oedipa puts the possibility that the Tristero may be a hoax on the same level as the fact of her own mortality, thus suggesting just how threatening it would be to her to discover that the Tristero was a figment of Pierce's imagination. She *needs* the Tristero to be "a real alternative" (H170.25) if she is not to be assumed back into the solipsism of her tower.

H168.22, B126.32 "If you need any armbands" Oedipa's bitter response links Fallopian's advice (harmless enough, on the face of it) to implications of fascistic control, suggesting that the hoax theory would entail a view of Pierce Inverarity very much in line with Jesús Arrabal's.

H169.1, B127.3 belly-up badger Essentially another version of the muted horn—a threat to the Thurn and Taxis monopoly, here represented by the badger, whose fur adorned the nose bands of the horses of the early couriers.

H169.1, B127.3 WE AWAIT SILENT TRISTERO'S EMPIRE The acronym's message points squarely to the possibility that is adumbrated in Bortz's Konrad scenario: the day may come when the Tristero becomes the dominant force, asserting its imperial power over a society whose outcasts will be different from those depicted in the novel.

H169.5, B127.8 a battered Scott catalogue The Scott catalog lists all stamps issued throughout the world and contains illustrations of many of them.

H169.8, B127.10 "An addendum" "She does not realize that Genghis Cohen is deliberately teasing her, kindling her paranoia. He is of course a member of the Tristero system, and he draws his pleasure from witnessing her hopeless attempts to penetrate the system" (Couturier 13). The reader can be forgiven for not sharing Couturier's certainty about Cohen's allegiance to an organization whose existence remains in doubt to the end.

H169.32, B127.31 waiting on something truly terrible While the immediate referent here appears to be the "unavoidable" realization that the whole Tristero legacy may be a fabrication of Inverarity's, the novel's characteristic ambiguity is sustained by the use of the word "waiting," which links "something" to "SILENT TRISTERO'S EMPIRE" and, later, to the breakdown of the "symmetry of choices" that comes to paralyze Oedipa near the end of the novel (H181.17n).

H170.17, B128.6 that afternoon's vanity mirror Watson notes the "narcissism implicit in conversing with a 'vanity mirror'" (70), but goes on to detail the parallel associations that link Oedipa with Echo, the other half of the Narcissus myth. The repetition of "either" in the sentences that follow reinforces Watson's claim that Narcissus and Echo represent the twin poles of Oedipa's dilemma over the Tristero: "Oedipa fears that, if she believes in the Tristero, she will prove to be Narcissus, mistaking the creations of her own confused perceptions for external reality. But if she refuses to believe in it, she risks discovering that it is a version of Echo, a real warning from an all-too-real creature which she . . . fails to heed" (71).

H170.18, B128.7 Either you have stumbled indeed This is perhaps the novel's most explicit evocation of the positive side of the Tristero, which here comes to represent true communication, as opposed to the "recitations of routine" that characterize our day-to-day exchanges with one another. The "exitlessness" that stands for the closed-system nature of our culture is linked here with "absence of surprise," reiterating the crucial juxtaposition of thermodynamics and information theory that forms the metaphorical heart of the novel.

H171.4, B128.26 it must have meaning An inkling of the more elaborate speculation Oedipa indulges in later over the possibility that Pierce might have devised "a plot . . . too elaborate for the dark Angel to hold at once" (H179.10n).

H171.9, B128.30 Those symmetrical four Which will soon be reduced to the binary symmetry of "twinned" ones and zeros in Oedipa's computer metaphor (H181.23).

H171.10, B128.31 hoped she was mentally ill Oedipa would clearly prefer at this stage to believe that there is no Tristero and that there is no plot—that she is simply "a nut." She is exhausted by the proliferation of signs, by the effort to establish meaning in a world that resolutely refuses to be pinned down. Mental illness, for all the uncertainty of vision that it implies, is nevertheless a fixed category, an explanation.

H171.13, B128.34 For this, oh God, was the void. Like the nothingness that haunted Mucho in his dream of the N.A.D.A. sign (H144.22n), and the void that the frail maidens in the tower attempt "hopelessly" to fill (H21.1n).

H171.31, B129.11 didn't show up for her next appointment "Perhaps she is subliminally unwilling to be the one who aborts Grace" (Watson 67).

H172.1, B129.14 the Royal Philatelic Society's The first important club devoted to philately, founded in 1869.

H172.5, B129.18 It was supposed to be The article's alleged inclusion in the authentic *Bibliothèque* lends it an authority that, as Seed points out, is called into question by the "hint of doubt" implicit in "supposed to be" (127).

H172.11, B129.23 Comte Raoul Antoine de Vouziers It would appear that Pynchon has made up this particular member of the family.

H172.27, B129.38 *the battle of Austerlitz* Fought on December 2, 1805, between French forces under Napoleon's command and a combined Austrian and Russian army. The battle resulted in a resounding victory for the smaller French force.

H172.27, B129.38 *the difficulties of 1848* The revolutions which swept Europe in that year in France, Italy, Germany, Austria, Bohemia, and Hungary.

H172.31, B130.2 *the ill-fated Frankfurt Assembly* The assembly was convened in 1848 by German nationalists who hoped to pave the way for German unification. "Ill-fated" because of the refusal of Czech nationalists, led by Frantisek Palacky, to participate (Stearns 110–11).

H172.32, B130.3 *in Buda-Pesth at the barricades* A bit enigmatic.

Perhaps a reference to the uprising in Budapest on March 15, 1848, when a crowd composed mostly of students stormed the citadel to release political prisoners.

H173.1, B130.4 *the watchmakers of the Jura* Within the flourishing Swiss labor movements of the mid-nineteenth century, the most radical group was formed by the mountain farmers/craftsmen of the villages of the Jura. Less well paid than their factory-based counterparts in urban centers such as Geneva, these independent-minded workers were ready to listen to the militant ideas of men such as Bakunin.

H173.2, B130.5 *the coming of M. Bakunin* Bakunin came to Geneva in 1867 and to LeLocle, in the Jura, in early 1869. His visit proved inspirational to the men of the Jura, who soon formed a splinter group, the Jura Fédération, that broke away from the larger Geneva-based Fédération Romande to pursue more clearly Bakuninist policies.

H173.9, B130.11 **the 1849 reaction** The aftermath of the European revolutions of 1848 assumed a variety of reactionary forms. In Germany, for example, voting laws were changed to ensure the election of a conservative parliament, while Prussian troops were dispatched to suppress the last vestiges of revolution wherever they flared up. Bakunin was among the victims of Prussian repression; he was arrested in Dresden and turned over to Russian authorities. Almost everywhere across Europe the story was the same. Last-ditch resistance by determined groups of revolutionaries, led, for example, by Kossuth in Hungary, Mazzini and Garibaldi in Italy, was brutally suppressed by Prussian, Russian, Austrian, and French troops. Constitutional reforms briefly enacted during the height of revolutionary successes were reversed or weakened by newly reinstated conservative governments (Stearns 185–222).

H173.12, B130.14 **Around 1845** See H54.1n for details of the various postal reform acts.

H174.9, B130.40 **Oedipa knew them by heart.** Oedipa has clearly been fascinated by what Mendelson calls a "delicate balance of the familiar and the unexpected," and her reluctance to pursue the lines of inquiry that continue to open up for her is no doubt attributable to the "powerful sense of menace and dread" produced by the stamps (130).

Nohrnberg notes that the forgeries represent "a losing battle against history, especially history of the official or panegyrical kind commemorated on postage stamps, of which the Tristero takes a satirist's cynical view" (152).

Decker singles out the Columbian Exposition forgery for particular mention, noting that it "implies . . . a challenge to U.S. nationalism's myth of origins. It satirizes conventional representations of America's beginnings, commenting critically on a mythic narrative. By implication, the stamp also challenges Frederick Jackson Turner's famous Frontier Thesis, delivered during the same 1893 World's Columbian Exposition in Chicago" (37).

It would appear that Pynchon consulted a stamp catalog when writing this passage, as all the stamps mentioned are real and as described, with the exception of the Tristero modifications. The airmail stamp on the sailor's letter was issued in July 1963.

H175.5, B131.26   The toothaches got worse   As Stimpson notes, Oedipa's "pregnancy" may herald the birth either of some redemptive process or of a threatening reinforcement of the isolation and stagnation that has characterized her life prior to Pierce's death (44). The unease and discomfort that increasingly accompanies her encounters with the trappings of the Tristero tend to emphasize the latter possibility.

H175.28, B132.7   "C. Morris Schrift"   *Schrift* is German for writing, prompting Berressem to infer that "future developments will involve further disseminations of texts, significations, and interpretations. The subject can be reached only *through* the 'agency of the letter'" (115).

H176.17, B132.27   drove on the freeway   Both Moddelmog (245) and Watson (64) note the Oedipal implications of Oedipa's decision to drive blind on the freeway. Watson adds the observation that those implications are reinforced by the tears that begin to "build up pressure around her eyes."

H177.19, B133.20   She had no more coins.   "The medium is again imposing its law, its logic upon the 'helpless' user, firing her with a desperate longing for communication which she can't appease" (Couturier 7).

H177.23, B133.23 she'd lost her bearings Her attempt to locate the sea recalls the earlier description of Oedipa's belief in the Pacific as "redemption" (H55.26). Here she has lost the capacity for such belief, a loss that is given added weight by her inability to locate the mountains which had, it appears, localized or contained the "ugliness" of her culture at the sea's edge. Now "the rest of the land" is included in the general indictment that lies at the heart of the novel's satire. San Narciso is no longer unique in its projection of all that is awry in Oedipa's world. The accompanying sense of loss, communicated with a poignant intensity by the description of the chime, is presumably occasioned by Oedipa's recognition, reiterated on the following page, that everything that San Narciso stands for is to be found in the rest of America also. Perhaps, too, whatever love may have been contained in the name of Pierce's city, whatever slight distinction may have been afforded by its association with her lover, has gone. Pierce is "really dead" and she is left only with the bitter insights afforded by her quest.

H178.8, B134.1 storm-systems . . . prevailing winds The extended metaphor continues Oedipa's insight of the previous page, her discovery of San Narciso's lack of uniqueness in a society where the weather patterns are driven by the "prevailing winds of affluence," which generate the "storm-systems of group suffering and need" that Oedipa has more and more become exposed to. The "tornado's touchdown" that is the city takes us back to her very first glimpse of it, when she sees "the ordered swirl of houses and streets" and feels that she is being communicated with "out of the eye of some whirlwind" (H24). The "true continuity" lies in San Narciso's being simply a part of the larger climatic pattern that is the legacy America.

H178.17, B134.9 having been by then too seized The novel's earlier references to epileptic seizures may provide the means for decoding this rather cryptic passage. Oedipa lists three possible causes for Pierce's lack of awareness of what is encrypted in his will:

"some headlong expansion of himself, some visit, some lucid instruction." The serial nature of the syntax allows for the possibility that Oedipa is describing a sequence of "events" that have taken place as a form of seizure. In this formulation, the will becomes the "secular announcement," the "compiled memories of clues, announcements, intimations" that is all that remains after the seizure (H95.10), and not "the central truth itself" that is here represented by the "lucid instruction" that is communicated to Pierce as a form of revelation, a "visit."

H178.28, B134.19 incommensurate with his need to possess Baxter (34) suggests an interesting parallel with the ending of *The Great Gatsby*, noting (in part) that the brief moment when man finds in the New World something "commensurate with his capacity for wonder" has given way to a world in which love, with its own share of wonder, cannot measure up to precisely the impulse that led to the destruction of the "fresh green breast" that becomes Pynchon's "most tender flesh" (H181.16).

Slade sees Inverarity's desire to transform the land as part of his "Calvinist approach to enterprise." Pierce is "the Protestant Ethic incarnate" (130).

H178.30, B134.21 "Keep it bouncing" Pierce's advice is central to the novel's concern with means of combating the energy degradation inherent in the functioning of closed systems. Like Nefastis, Pierce sees the need "to keep it all cycling."

H179.10, B134.33 had a plot finally been devised Oedipa may well be thinking at this moment of the lesson she learns from her encounter with the old sailor. While the destruction of the mattress would be sufficient to eradicate even the memory of the men who had slept on it, Pierce may have devised a way to prevent such an eradication in his own case. The complex chemical encodings that Oedipa envisages having been imprinted on the mattress are simple in comparison with the elaborate matrix of interconnected signs that Pierce may have created as a means of "beating" death.

Just what it means to survive as "a paranoia" is not immediately clear, however. If Pierce has indeed fabricated the whole Tristero as a plot against Oedipa, then who is being paranoid? Although the syntax establishes an equivalence between "a paranoia" and "a pure conspiracy," the two are presumably exclusive of one another, since one can scarcely be paranoid about a real conspiracy.

H179.22, B135.4 she might have found The Tristero anywhere As is typical throughout the novel, the possible significance of one of Oedipa's insights is undermined by its being expressed conditionally. If "there really was a Tristero," then. . . . Nevertheless, the recognition that a transformative vision of one's world may be available only just beyond the threshold of the day-to-day is bound to carry some weight, even if its complete validation is dependent on a truth that cannot be established.

Mendelson clearly wishes to attach some religious significance to this moment, citing Eliade's description of the threshold (here the "lightly-concealed entranceways") as "the limit, the boundary, the frontier that distinguishes and opposes two worlds—and at the same time the paradoxical place where those two worlds communicate, where passage from the profane to the sacred becomes possible" (132).

H179.29, B135.11 knowing they . . . authenticated the great night Perhaps Oedipa is once again experiencing a sense of her connectedness to all those aspects of "her Republic" that she has hitherto either ignored or been unconscious of. This feeling manifested itself earlier in her instinctive embrace of the drunken sailor and now is broadened by the imagined network of rail lines to encompass the whole legacy America that Oedipa dimly senses may be her heritage. The "great night," which "the Word" was to have abolished (H118.16n), is now "authenticated" by a spirit of mutuality.

On the other hand, one might argue that the rail lines, with their "hard, strung presence," represent the stranglehold of mainstream, inflexible ideas, which deepen the night and authenticate in the sense of validate it, leaving off to one side, down abandoned branch lines, those members of the human community deemed unfit for inclusion.

H180.5, B135.20 as perhaps Oedipa one day might have The unspoken completion of this sentence—"had she not . . ."—suggests that Oedipa has arrived at a point of no return. She "might have" forgotten, had she not been so far taken up by the implications of her discoveries that she will never be able to dismiss the Tristero, real or not, from her consciousness.

H180.7, B135.22 She thought of other, immobilized Oedipa's memories bring to the foreground those figures whom our culture tends to marginalize and render invisible. Although she recognizes the distance that separates these figures from the mainstream, she also senses their connection to it; hence, the freight cars are immobilized, the lean-tos are erected behind the billboards, the cars are junked, the lineman's tent is strung in the copper rigging but entails no commitment to or concern for the "unheard messages" that constitute the "secular miracle of communication." Rejected by, or choosing to opt out of, mainstream culture, these squatters and drifters are nevertheless "congruent" with the land that Oedipa has lived in all her life, as San Narciso is part of a larger, newly discovered continuity.

Seed has some reservations about the passage, arguing that its tone is "too categorical" and that it "suggests an actual community whereas the novel as a whole has constantly rendered any reference to the Tristero as problematic" (149). He also thinks that "the secular miracle" is devoid of irony, and thus "out of key in a novel at pains to demonstrate the *difficulty* of communicating." I think this fails to take into account the fact, already noted, that the adventurous squatters who pass their nights in the linemen's tent are "untroubled" by the secular communications that flash along the wires. By association, they are linked with all those who are "searching" for the "magical Other" who is to be the "trigger" that will bring into this world the "Word" that represents the influx of energy from outside so necessary to rejuvenate our culture. The use of "herself" here strongly suggests that Oedipa unconsciously admits the possibility that she may be that trigger.

H181.9, B136.14 administrator *de bonis non* Administrator, that is, of the goods not settled—of the remainder of the estate.

H181.10, B136.15 so much baby for code Oedipa knows full well how much separates her now from the ordinary world of common sense, of probate, of letters testamentary. Her speculation that she might be "hounded" into joining the Tristero, presumably by the putative derision of the probate judge, seems to situate her on the less rational side of the divide.

H181.17, B136.22 waiting for a symmetry of choices to break down
Oedipa's uneasiness with the binary choices that she sees confronting her is a measure of her understanding of the dangers represented by either/or thinking. The absolutism of the choices— either transcendent meaning or no meaning at all—excludes the possibility of undecidable propositions which would connote precisely the diversity that has been leached out of American life (Kharpertian 86). Oedipa needs the uncertainty that constitutes the excluded middle of her predicament if she is to be able to follow Pierce's advice and "keep it bouncing." To choose either the one or the zero in any of the pairs that she describes would be to put an end to the quest that has kept her out of the confining tower of her previous life. Nicholson compares Oedipa's willingness to remain open to possibilities other than the binary pairs that oppress her to Keats's state of negative capability (104).

Mendelson focuses more squarely on the significance of the ones and zeros, arguing that "the religious content of the book is fixed in Oedipa's dilemma: the choice between the *zero* of secular triviality and chaos, and the *one* which is the *ganz andere* of the sacred" (130).

H182.11, B137.6 the only way she could continue There can be no return for Oedipa to the furrow of conventional life in Kinneret. She now stands permanently outside her former experience and will be able to live in "just America" only if she can believe in the possibilities represented by the Tristero, which she must create for herself if it turns out that it has no independent existence.

H183.1, B137.27 "Loren Passerine" As Watson notes, Passerine's name refers to an order of birds, one that "includes the passerine ground-dove" (69), beginning the many associations with Pentecost developed in this closing scene.

H183.2, B137.27 "crying" In the auction of the Tristero stamps, Nohrnberg sees a kind of circularity, suggesting that the "crying" of lot 49 is analogous to the "aboriginal" scene that must have taken place at some time prior to the beginning of the novel, namely the reading of Pierce's will (158).

H183.6, B137.31 "Your fly is open" Cohen appears to be a consistently sloppy dresser. His fly is half open when Oedipa first meets him (H94.27). On the assumption that Cohen may in fact be part of the Tristero conspiracy, Hunt sees Oedipa's remark as evidence of "a lightness of touch, a humorous self-critical disposition, a *joie de vivre*, which saves [Oedipa] almost to the last from the insanity she comes desperately to hope explains the connections she sees" (38). Slade, too, regards the humor as "redeeming," claiming that Pynchon introduces it "to soften his heroine's terror and to suggest that the alternatives are endless and exciting" (175).

H183.8, B137.33 causing a scene Watson is reminded of the scene in Hitchcock's *North by Northwest,* in which Cary Grant "bids fiercely for an unwanted lot, hoping to gain enough attention from the public and the police to protect him from the men he believes are there to kill him as well as to bid themselves" (73).

H183.11, B137.36 rising and falling points of dust A reminder, perhaps, through the suggestion of the randomness of Brownian motion, of the necessary chaos of the alternative world that Oedipa is being forced to confront. The old stabilities of her previous existence have given way to a recognition of the culture's need for a new complexity of vision.

H183.14, B137.38 "It's time to start" Opinions about the final scene differ largely in terms of the weight given the religious associations that are undeniably present. Critics note the link with Pentecost that is forged by the number 49, and they note the way in which that link reinforces the novel's deferral of closure. Tanner's reading is more or less representative: "As Edward Mendelson has pointed out, 49 is the pentecostal number (the Sunday seven weeks after Easter), but Pentecost derives from the Greek for 'fifty,' so the moment at the end of the book when the auctioneer's spread arms are specifically likened to 'a gesture . . . culture' is like the moment before a pentecostal revelation when we would all be able to speak in tongues—and be able to understand 'the Word' directly"

("Crying" 185–86). Mendelson suggests that the deferral of revelation is an indication of the sacred nature of the experience Oedipa has undergone: "A manifestation of the sacred can only be believed in; it can never be proved beyond doubt" (134). Others push in the direction of more secular readings: "This ending projects one beyond the terms of the book by indicating the degree to which silence (the inarticulacy of the dispossessed?) is more important and potent than language. The text cannot speak the Other: to do so would be to coopt it, to destroy it by bringing it to the light" (Coates 128). "The fact that no revelation concludes the book, that it exists only in potential, fits the thematic design. An absolute answer would end the flow of information, replacing the ambiguity that is indigenous to postmodern realism with a certainty which would maximize entropy" (87).

Watson points out that the "descending angel" image is more closely linked with the idea of annunciation than with that of Pentecost: "The implied visitation of the Holy Ghost might refer to His descent to impregnate Mary rather than to his descent to plant new speech in the Disciples. If we accept the notion that Oedipa will, to her own shock, turn out to be the Tristero bidder, then the possibilities are not mutually exclusive. Oedipa's gestation of a new, Tristero self, the Annunciation of the meaning of that pregnancy, and her Pentecostal moment of finding unexpected foreign speech on her tongue, all culminate together when Oedipa finds herself bidding for the Tristero" (69).

References

Abernethy, Peter. "Entropy in Pynchon's *The Crying of Lot 49*." *Critique* 14, no. 2 (1972): 18–33.

Arnheim, Rudolf. *Entropy and Art: An Essay on Disorder and Order.* Berkeley and Los Angeles: University of California Press, 1971.

Barthelme, Donald. *Snow White.* New York: Bantam, 1967.

Bassoff, Bruce. "De-faced America: *The Great Gatsby* and *The Crying of Lot 49*." *Pynchon Notes* 7 (October 1981): 22–37.

Bennett, Charles H. "Demons, Engines and the Second Law." *Scientific American*, November 1987, 108–16.

Bennett, David. "Parody, Postmodernism, and the Politics of Reading." *Critical Quarterly* 27, no. 4 (Winter 1985): 27–43.

Berressem, Hanjo. *Pynchon's Poetics.* Urbana and Chicago: University of Illinois Press, 1993.

Bloom, Harold, ed. *Thomas Pynchon: Modern Critical Views.* New York: Chelsea House, 1986.

Bolton, William. *Patterns in Physics.* New York: McGraw Hill, 1974.

Brillouin, L. "Maxwell's Demon Cannot Operate: Information and Entropy. I." In *Maxwell's Demon*, ed. Leff and Rex, 134–37.

Buxton, Frank, and Bill Owen. *Radio's Golden Age.* New York: Easton Valley Press, 1966.

Caesar, Terry P. "A Note on Pynchon's Naming." *Pynchon Notes* 5 (February 1981): 5–10.

Cammaerts, Emile. *A History of Belgium.* New York: D. Appleton, 1921.

Castillo, Debra A. "Borges and Pynchon: The Tenuous Symmetries of Art." In *New Essays*, ed. O'Donnell, 21–46.

Chambers, Judith. *Thomas Pynchon.* New York: Twayne Publishers, 1992.

Coates, Paul. "Unfinished Business: Thomas Pynchon and the Quest for Revolution." *New Left Review* 160 (November–December 1986): 122–28.

Colville, Georgiana M. *Beyond and Beneath the Mantle: On Thomas Pynchon's "The Crying of Lot 49."* Amsterdam: Rodopi, 1988.

Conroy, Mark. "The American Way and Its Double in *The Crying of Lot 49*." *Pynchon Notes* 24–25 (Spring–Fall 1989): 45–70.

Cooper, Peter L. *Signs and Symptoms: Thomas Pynchon and the Contemporary World.* Berkeley and Los Angeles: University of California Press, 1983.

Couturier, Maurice. "The Death of the Real in *The Crying of Lot 49*." *Pynchon Notes* 20–21 (1987): 5–29.

Cowart, David. "Pynchon's *The Crying of Lot 49* and the Paintings of Remedios Varo." *Critique* 18, no. 3 (1977): 19–26.

———. *Thomas Pynchon: The Art of Allusion.* Carbondale: Southern Illinois University Press, 1980.

Das, Prasanta. "Oedipa's Night Journey in Pynchon's *The Crying of Lot 49*." *Notes on Contemporary Literature* 23, no. 2 (1993): 4–5.

Davidson, Cathy N. "Oedipa as Androgyne in Thomas Pynchon's *The Crying of Lot 49*." *Contemporary Literature* 18 (Winter 1977): 38–50.

Daw, Laurence. "Banishing the Pesky Demon: The Final Word." *Pynchon Notes* 22–23 (1988): 99–101.

Decker, Jeffrey Louis. "'The Enigma His Efforts Had Created': Thomas Pynchon and the Legacy of America." *Pynchon Notes* 28–29 (Spring–Fall 1991).

Delepinne, Berthe. *Histoire de La Poste Internationale en Belgique sous les grands maîtres des postes de la famille de Tassis.* Brussels: Wellens and Godenne, 1952.

Denbigh, K. "How Subjective Is Entropy?" In *Maxwell's Demon*, ed. Leff and Rex, 109–15.

Denbigh, K. G., and J. S. Denbigh. *Entropy in Relation to Incomplete Knowledge.* Cambridge: Cambridge University Press, 1985.

Dugdale, J. V. *Thomas Pynchon: Allusive Parables of Power.* New York: St. Martin's, 1990.

Duyfhuizen, Bernard. "'Hushing Sick Transmissions': Disrupting Story in *The Crying of Lot 49*." In *New Essays*, ed. O'Donnell, 79–96.

Eddins, Dwight. *The Gnostic Pynchon.* Bloomington: Indiana University Press, 1990.

Engel, Peter. "Against the Currents of Chaos." *Sciences* 24 (September–October 1984): 50–55.

Fowler, Douglas. "Epilepsy as Metaphor in *The Crying of Lot 49.*" *Notes on Contemporary Literature* 14, no. 2 (1984): 10–12.

Gatlin, Lila L. *Information Theory and the Living System.* New York: Columbia University Press, 1972.

Grace, Sherrill. "Wastelands and Badlands: The Legacies of Pynchon and Kroetsch." *Mosaic* 14, no. 2 (1981): 20–34.

Green, Martin. "*The Crying of Lot 49:* Pynchon's Heart of Darkness." *Pynchon Notes* 8 (February 1982): 30–38.

Guzlowski, John. "*The Crying of Lot 49* and 'The Shadow.' " *Pynchon Notes* 9 (June 1982): 61–68.

Haldi, John. *Postal Monopoly: An Assessment of the Private Express Statutes.* Washington: American Enterprise Institute for Public Policy Research, 1974.

Hall, Chris. " 'Behind the Hieroglyphic Streets': Pynchon's Oedipa Maas and the Dialectics of Reading." *Critique* 33 (Fall 1991): 63–72.

Harlow, Alvin F. *Old Post Bags.* New York: Appleton and Co., 1928.

Hartley, R. V. L. "Transmission of Information." *Bell System Technical Journal* 7, no. 3 (July 1928): 535–63.

Hayles, N. Katherine. " 'A Metaphor of God Knew How Many Parts': The Engine That Drives *The Crying of Lot 49.*" In *New Essays,* ed. O'Donnell, 97–125.

Henkle, Roger B. "Pynchon's Tapestries on the Western Wall." In *Collection of Critical Essays,* ed. Mendelson, 97–111.

Hite, Molly. *Ideas of Order in the Novels of Thomas Pynchon.* Columbus: Ohio State University Press, 1983.

Hollander, Charles. "Pynchon's Politics: The Presence of an Absence." *Pynchon Notes* 26–27 (Spring–Fall 1990): 5–59.

Irwin, Mark. "A Note on 'Porky Pig and the Anarchist' in *The Crying of Lot 49* and *Gravity's Rainbow.*" *Pynchon Notes* 28–29 (Spring–Fall 1991): 55–57.

Johnston, John. "Toward the Schizo-Text: Paranoia as Semiotic Regime in *The Crying of Lot 49.*" In *New Essays,* ed. O'Donnell, 47–78.

Kaplan, Janet. *The Art and Life of Remedios Varo.* New York: Abbeville Press, 1988.

Kermode, Frank. "The Use of Codes in *The Crying of Lot 49.*" In *Modern Critical Views,* ed. Bloom, 11–14.

Kharpertian, Theodore D. *A Hand to Turn the Time: The Menippean Satires of Thomas Pynchon.* Rutherford, N.J.: Fairleigh Dickinson University Press, 1990.

Kolodny, Annette, and Daniel James Peters. "Pynchon's *The Crying of Lot 49:* The Novel as Subversive Experience." *Modern Fiction Studies* 19 (Spring 1973): 79–87.

Landauer, Rolf. "Irreversibility and Heat Generation in the Computing Process." In *Maxwell's Demon,* ed. Leff and Rex, 188–96.

Langland, Elizabeth. *Society in the Novel.* Chapel Hill: University of North Carolina Press, 1984.

Leff, Harvey S., and Andrew F. Rex. *Maxwell's Demon: Entropy, Information, Computing.* Princeton, N.J.: Princeton University Press, 1990.

Leland, John P. "Pynchon's Linguistic Demon: *The Crying of Lot 49.*" *Critique* 16, no. 2 (1974): 45–53.

Levine, George, and David Leverenz. *Mindful Pleasures: Essays on Thomas Pynchon.* Boston: Little, Brown, 1976.

Mac Adam, Alfred. "Pynchon as Satirist: To Write, To Mean." *Yale Review* 67, no. 4 (1978): 555–66.

McHoul, Alec. "Telegrammatology, Part I: *Lot 49* and the Post-ethical." *Pynchon Notes* 18–19 (Spring–Fall 1986): 39–54.

McHoul, Alec, and David Wills. *Writing Pynchon: Strategies in Fictional Analysis.* Urbana: University of Illinois Press, 1990.

Mackey, Douglas A. *The Rainbow Quest of Thomas Pynchon.* San Bernadino: Borgo Press, 1980.

Madsen, Deborah L. *The Postmodernist Allegories of Thomas Pynchon.* New York: St. Martin's Press, 1991.

Mangel, Anne. "Maxwell's Demon, Entropy, Information: *The Crying of Lot 49.*" *TriQuarterly* 20 (Winter 1971): 194–208.

Mendelson, Edward. "The Sacred, the Profane, and *The Crying of Lot 49.*" In *Pynchon: A Collection of Critical Essays,* ed. Mendelson, 97–111. Englewood Cliffs, N.J.: Prentice-Hall, 1978.

Merrill, Robert. "The Form and Meaning of Pynchon's *The Crying of Lot 49.*" *Ariel: A Review of International English Literature* 8, no. 1 (1977): 53–71.

Moddelmog, Debra A. "The Oedipus Myth and Reader Response in Pynchon's *The Crying of Lot 49.*" *Papers on Language and Literature* 23 (Spring 1987): 240–49.

Moorhead, Alan. *Gallipoli.* New York: Harper and Brothers, 1956.

Newman, Robert D. *Understanding Thomas Pynchon.* Columbia: University of South Carolina Press, 1986.

Nicholson, C. E., and R. W. Stevenson. " 'Words You Never Wanted to Hear':

Fiction, History and Narratology in *The Crying of Lot 49.*" *Pynchon Notes* 16 (1985): 89–109.

Nohrnberg, James. "Pynchon's Paraclete." In *Collection of Critical Essays*, ed. Mendelson, 147–61.

O'Donnell, Patrick, ed. *New Essays on "The Crying of Lot 49."* New York: Cambridge University Press, 1991.

Olsen, Lance. *Ellipse of Uncertainty: An Introduction to Postmodern Fantasy.* New York: Greenwood, 1987.

Palmeri, Frank. "Neither Literally nor as Metaphor: Pynchon's *The Crying of Lot 49* and the Structure of Scientific Revolutions." *ELH* 54 (1987): 979–99.

Pearce, Richard. "Where're They At, Where're They Going? Thomas Pynchon and the American Novel in Motion." In *Essays on Thomas Pynchon*, ed. Pearce, 213–29. Boston: G. K. Hall, 1981.

Petillon, Pierre-Yves. "A Re-cognition of Her Errand into the Wilderness." In *New Essays*, ed. O'Donnell, 127–70.

Plater, William M. *The Grim Phoenix: Reconstructing Thomas Pynchon.* Bloomington: Indiana University Press, 1978.

Poirier, Richard. "The Importance of Thomas Pynchon." In *Mindful Pleasures*, ed. Levine and Leverenz, 15–30.

Pütz, Manfred. "The Art of the Acronym in Thomas Pynchon." *Studies in the Novel* 23, no. 3 (Fall 1991): 371–82.

Pynchon, Thomas. *The Crying of Lot 49.* New York: Harper and Row, 1986.

———. "Entropy." *Kenyon Review* (Spring 1960): 277–92.

———. "Low-lands." In Gregory Fitzgerald, ed. *The Impropriety Principle.* Glennview, Ill.: Scott, Foresman and Co., 1971. 224–44.

———. *Slow Learner.* Boston: Little, Brown, 1984.

———. *V.* Harmondsworth: Penguin Books, 1966.

Richwell, Adrian Emily. "*The Crying of Lot 49:* A Source Study." *Pynchon Notes* 17 (Fall 1985): 78–80.

———. "Pynchon's *The Crying of Lot 49.*" *Explicator* 47, no. 1 (Fall 1988): 50–52.

Rodd, P. "Some Comments on Entropy and Information." In *Maxwell's Demon*, ed. Leff and Rex, 145–47.

Rothstein, J. "Information, Measurement, and Quantum Mechanics." In *Maxwell's Demon*, ed. Leff and Rex, 104–8.

Rundle, Vivienne. "The Double Bind of Metafiction: Implicating Narrative in *The Crying of Lot 49* and *Travesty.*" *Pynchon Notes* 24–25 (Spring–Fall 1989): 32–44.

Schaub, Thomas Hill. "Open Letter in Response to Edward Mendelson's 'The Sacred, The Profane, and *The Crying of Lot 49*.'" *Boundary 2* 4 (Fall 1976): 93–101.

———. *Pynchon: The Voice of Ambiguity*. Urbana: University of Illinois Press, 1981.

Seed, David. *The Fictional Labyrinths of Thomas Pynchon*. Iowa City: University of Iowa Press, 1988.

Shannon, C. E. "A Mathematical Theory of Communication." *Bell System Technical Journal* 27, no. 3 (July 1948): 379–423.

Slade, Joseph W. *Thomas Pynchon*. New York: Warner Paperback Library, 1974.

Stearns, Peter. *1848: The Revolutionary Tide in Europe*. New York: Norton, 1974.

Sterling, Christopher H., and John M. Kittross. *Stay Tuned*. Belmont, Calif.: Wadsworth, 1978.

Stimpson, Catherine R. "Pre-Apocalyptic Atavism: Thomas Pynchon's Early Fiction." In *Mindful Pleasures*, ed. Levine and Leverenz, 31–47. Reprinted in *Modern Critical Views*, ed. Bloom, 79–81.

Szilard, L. "On the Decrease of Entropy in a Thermodynamic System by the Intervention of Intelligent Beings." In *Maxwell's Demon*, ed. Leff and Rex, 124–33.

Tanner, Tony. *City of Words*. London: Jonathan Cape, 1971.

———. "*The Crying of Lot 49*." In *Modern Critical Views*, ed. Bloom, 175–89.

———. *Thomas Pynchon*. London: Methuen, 1982.

———. "V. and V-2." In *Collection of Critical Essays*, ed. Mendelson, 16–55.

Temkin, Owsei. *The Falling Sickness*. Baltimore: Johns Hopkins University Press, 1971.

Tyson, Lois. "Existential Subjectivity on Trial: *The Crying of Lot 49* and the Politics of Despair." *Pynchon Notes* 28–29 (Spring–Fall 1991): 5–25.

Watson, Robert N. "Who Bids for Tristero? The Conversion of Pynchon's Oedipa Maas." *Southern Humanities Review* 17 (Winter 1983): 59–75.

Weisenburger, Steven. *A Gravity's Rainbow Companion*. Athens, Georgia: University of Georgia Press, 1988.

Wiener, Norbert. *The Human Use of Human Beings*. London: Sphere Books, 1968.

Winston, Matthew. "A Comic Source of *Gravity's Rainbow*." *Pynchon Notes* 15 (Fall 1984): 73–76.

Index

Index entries are keyed to the references to the Perennial Library edition of *The Crying of Lot 49* that appear in the text. Roman numeral citations refer to page numbers in the introduction of the present volume.

Prof.
zimian